To Fiona
with love

The
Gravy Train

Philip Bushill-Matthews (signature)

Philip Bushill-Matthews

Polperro Heritage Press

© Philip Bushill-Matthews 2003

ISBN 0-9544233-2-1

Published by
Polperro Heritage Press
Clifton-upon-Teme
Worcestershire WR6 6EN
polperro.press@virgin.net

Printed by Orphans Press
Leominster HR6 8JT
United Kingdom

Cover design: Steve Bowgen

MEPs are the most pampered politicians in the world. They are all on the gravy train.

Just about everybody

Who are our MEPs anyway? Who chose them in the first place, and what on earth do they do?

Just about everybody else

Anyone seen my husband?

Angela Bushill-Matthews

Foreword

In 1999 the British people faced an important choice on the future of Europe. Unlike other political parties the Conservative Party did not believe that handing over sovereignty to Europe was an inevitability. Instead we held to our belief that Britain should be 'In Europe, not run by Europe.'

The British people agreed. They told Tony Blair that political institutions matter, that national identity matters and democratic accountability matters. They told the Prime Minister that too many powers had been handed over to unelected bureaucrats and Europe should concentrate on doing less and doing it better.

The result was that in 1999 the Conservative Party doubled its number of Members of the European Parliament. British Conservatives would now be sending 36 MEPs to Brussels. But just what exactly were these MEPs going to do in Brussels once they arrived? And what difference can 36 people make in an assembly of 626?

Among the new members of the European Parliament was Philip Bushill-Matthews. This account of his life and experiences as an MEP is a first hand look at how a local businessman can become a Member of the European Parliament inside 14 months, what he can do when he's there and even what expenses and salary he is entitled to!

This book looks in detail at many aspects of the real life of an MEP from fraud-busting to expense-claiming, and from coping with constituents to coping with reams of red tape. It shows how MEPs have to deal with whole rafts of legislation from the debate on the European Constitution to the directive on how to climb a ladder.

Philip explains in an easy to read, light-hearted way what it is like to become an MEP and what difference individual MEPs can make to important legislation. But, above all, *The Gravy Train* demonstrates the importance of electing a candidate with previous experience of real life and a candidate who will work hard to forge a better, more accountable Europe.

I pay tribute to my colleagues in the European Parliament for the work they have done to improve European legislation, and to hold off the relentless march towards a single European superstate. Long may they continue to do so.

Rt Hon William Hague MP

Acknowledgements

There are many people I must thank, without whom this book would not have been possible:

- the hundreds of thousands of West Midlands electors who all put their crosses in the Right box at the 1999 European Election;

- the hundreds of Tory hyper-activists who spurred them to do it;

- Tony Blair, who proposed the current daft system of proportional representation, without which I could never have become selected or elected in the first place;

- the 29 Labour MEPs who have consistently handed me so much ammunition to fire back at them;

- my 35 Conservative MEP colleagues who have taught me so much;

- specifically the Tory West Midlands MEP team, who have combined to make a tireless Gang of Four;

- the Stratford Conservative Patrons Club and other friendly folk, who have helped defray publication costs;

- above all my dear wife Angela, without whose unflagging energy and selfless support I could have never committed to the role, let alone have intruded further into our limited time together to write a book about it.

Contents

Foreword
Acknowledgements

Chapter One

From Pork Scratchings to Politics

I have never been keen on politicians. They have a lousy image, and many deserve it.

The idea that I might aspire to become one never occurred to me. I had been in business for some thirty years, was still enjoying it, and still learning. But in 1997 my wife Angela and I decided to celebrate our thirtieth Wedding Anniversary by doing something really romantic – attending our first Conservative Party Conference.

Blackpool in October is not the most alluring venue. It was cold and soulless. The Press was expecting the conference atmosphere to be the same, since the Conservatives had just lost the General Election, but inside the conference hall everyone was looking to the future in a remarkably positive way. The enthusiasm was infectious, and I found myself caught up in it. On the spur of the moment, I decided to put my name on the list of possible speakers for one of the debates. There was much talk of the need for change, even changing the name of the party itself, and that had given me an idea.

As I mounted the platform for my two minutes of fame and suggested that the party should think of a different name for the 1922 Committee, I still had no thought of a career change. Even so, my maiden speech had gone down rather well, though my contribution had been put in proper perspective by the Chairman who introduced me with: "I now call on Philip Bushill-Matthews, to be followed by Jeffrey Archer." A buzz that went round the hall was not for me. The BBC immediately switched its coverage from the stage for a quick interview with William Waldegrave in order to be back in time for Jeffrey.

My big moment might have been small, but it was fun. After it was over, several things happened in quick succession which were to change my life.

At the conference I was appalled to discover how few MPs out of 659 in the previous Parliament had ever had previous manufacturing business experience. There were only five. Most MPs were lawyers, teachers, journalists or simply career politicians with no first-hand knowledge of the real world. Little wonder, I thought, that manufacturers were being slowly strangled by regulation. Most of the lawmakers had no idea they were creating more problems than they were solving. If only there were more politicians with a business background. Then we might get some sanity.

I bumped into Dame Rachel Dyche, Midlands Regional Director for the Conservatives, and asked her why more business people didn't go into politics.

"Because people like you don't put your name forward," came the obvious reply. But still the penny didn't drop that it had anything to do with me. The idea of being a Westminster MP had zero appeal. Parliament seemed so much like a children's debating society. Anyway, to serve a long political apprenticeship in order to get a winnable seat, then find you were powerless in Opposition or ignored on the back-benches even when one's party was in Government, had never tempted me for an instant.

Then I met Veronica Stiastny, a former neighbour when we lived in Surrey. She proudly announced that she had become a county councillor in order to strengthen her CV with a view to becoming a Member of the European Parliament.

It may sound ridiculous, but suddenly I realised that was what I wanted to do. Europe was where the action was, not Westminster. In Brussels there was no Opposition, because there was no Government. There were no backbenchers, because there were no front-benchers. Each of the 626 MEPs across the fifteen Member States had an equal and immediate opportunity to promote or amend legislation, or indeed call for less of it. If I wanted to do something about over-regulation then here was a real opportunity.

I raced back to Rachel Dyche to ask her what she thought.

"Go for it," she said without hesitation.

I wondered how to broach this with my wife. When I did, she told me she already knew. She had listened to me speaking from the platform about the 1922 committee and immediately realised: "My God! He is going into politics!" She knew before I did. I wish she had told me.

She also said I should go for it, but we consoled ourselves that it was a very long shot.

The following week I wrote off for the application form, which had to be countersigned by an MP (our local MP John Maples gladly obliged) and a constituency Chairman. My local Chairman Don Rushton agreed to sign in principle but said he wanted to hear me speak about Europe first. A local meeting was called with myself set up as the speaker. After it was over, Don simply asked: "Where do I sign?"

The application was sent off, and accepted. I was then called for my first interview – before Rachel Dyche! After a thorough grilling about my motivation and my experience, she was generous with her support.

Next stop was an interview with Lord Freeman in London. I had expected this to be a tough session, but it turned out to be a relatively easy ride. The biggest test was however still to come: a full two-day selection board.

Before that took place I spoke to John Corrie, the sitting Conservative MEP for Worcestershire and South Warwickshire. He had kindly invited me to Brussels to see what it was like on the inside, though he was well aware that I could be competing against him if I was selected as a candidate.

In the course of two exhilarating days. I was shown round the Parliament, allowed into one of the committees in session, and introduced to a large number of MEPs, British and other nationalities. John and I also had dinner with Edward McMillan Scott, the current leader of the Conservative MEPs, who I found immensely impressive.

When I eventually arrived for the weekend selection board, the first person I met was Veronica Stiastny.

"What on earth are you doing here?" she asked.

I told her it was all her fault.

The selection board process for Conservative candidates for the European Parliament is modelled on the Nazi officer assessment course that has been used as a template for army and big business recruitment in the UK for many years. I had been through a similar ordeal years earlier when I applied to join Unilever as a management trainee. With a series of role-plays in small groups of eight sitting in a small circle, with existing MEPs watching in judgement in an outer ring, it was just as much an ordeal this time around.

One week later I was told I had passed. Just three months had gone by since the Party Conference, and I was already an approved prospective MEP candidate. Everything I had learned in my 30-year career in business suddenly assumed a new perspective. At the time I was Managing Director of Red Mill Snack Foods in Wednesbury, and of a sister company in the Netherlands. The UK business was the larger of the two, with a wider product range that included the well-known Black Country delicacy Mr Porky pork scratchings.

It was big business, but I had become increasingly frustrated with the mounting tide of regulations. The regulations for fire extinguishers, for example, changed as a result of an EU Directive on Health and Safety. For years we had fire extinguishers painted in different colours (red, black, cream etc.,) for electrical, chemical or gas fires. If a fire broke out suddenly, you needed to grab the right one instantly, otherwise you could end up feeding the fire instead of putting it out. The new rules required all extinguishers to be red, with just a discreet coloured badge in the middle to indicate the different contents. The changes were costly and misguided but we were stuck with them.

Then came more Health and Safety regulations. Successive local inspectors had their own interpretation of what modifications we had to make to conform with the regulations. Their requirements were often unreasonable and seldom necessary. But their word was absolute.

Soon we were also blessed with the Working Time Directive, a supreme piece of EU social engineering that masqueraded as a Health and Safety measure. We didn't want it and our employees didn't want it either. As a 24-hour production operation, making a short shelf-life product with fluctuating consumer demand, the business needed particular flexibility over working time, and the 300-plus workforce was happy to provide it. We believed in working together in harmony, but we were nevertheless all stuck with the Directive. As a result, we were almost overwhelmed by the mountain of paperwork that had to be completed for each individual member of staff, recording work time, break time and travel time – all to be filed carefully for at least six years.

I was later to learn that EU Directives have to be transposed into national legislation before they become law, and the UK holds the European record for embellishing and embroidering them with prescriptive details that were never suggested in the original Directive. British MPs assume there is no point in challenging what is ordained in Brussels, while MEPs had no cause to follow up what happened to Directives once these had passed through the European Parliament.

When the Working Time Directive came out I wrote to the Dutch Government for guidance in my capacity as Managing Director of Red Mill Company BV. They sent me eight pages of notes, all were really quite sensible. I also wrote to the UK Government, to receive 134 pages in reply; attached was a covering letter saying that I could expect to receive a fuller briefing in due course when certain details had been resolved in the courts.

I had been getting thoroughly fed up with all this excessive regulation. For a company of our size, it was a burden we could well do without. And I knew that others shared my frustration and yearned to do something about it.

I also knew that it was going to get worse. One of Tony Blair's earliest decisions after winning the General Election in 1997 was to sign up to the EU Social Chapter. As a result, businesses were going to be deluged with progressively more legislation, with companies compelled to shed staff in order to contain rising costs. If only something could be done.

At that stage it had not occurred to me that I could play any role in doing it. The idea of entering the political arena myself had never entered my head. Although a paid-up member of the Conservative party, my political experience had essentially been limited to campaigning for a 'yes' vote during the 1975 referendum on remaining in the EEC and working with my local Conservative Association in Stratford-on-Avon. I was too busy pursuing my career, doing a job that I enjoyed.

Suddenly, all that was about to change. Or was it? As an 'approved' candidate I was only at the bottom rung of the political ladder. I still needed to find a seat, and then get elected.

When it came to choosing where to stand, I decided that my home region was the only one to go for. I had been born in Worcestershire, raised in Birmingham, worked in the Black Country and lived in Warwickshire. Overall I had spent half my life in the West Midlands. If my home region wouldn't have me, I felt I had no right to stand anywhere else.

The selection process for MEPs was going to be very different for all the candidates this time around. In the past, individual MEPs had been selected to stand in individual constituencies, the successful candidate winning under the traditional first-past-the-post system. In the West Midlands there were eight MEPs, seven of whom were currently Labour. But Tony Blair had decided to change the system so that he could better control the selection process and weed out Labour MEPs he disapproved of. There would still be eight MEPs in the region, but the eight would now share the region as one giant collective constituency. Each political party would each choose eight candidates of their own: the lists would then be offered to the electorate who would have one vote for a party slate rather than an individual MEP.

The Conservatives hated this new system, maintaining it was undemocratic. Individual constituencies wanted their own individual MEP. Voters wanted to know who they were voting for, and whom they could hold to account. But Tony Blair had decided, and that was that.

As the votes would be applied on a proportional representation system, the outcome would be to some extent predictable. The Liberal Democrats should get one, Conservatives three or four, and Labour four or three. This meant that if I could somehow get pre-selected in a high enough position, I would be home. Second place behind our only existing Conservative MEP in the West Midlands would suit me fine, but there would surely be other candidates with a much stronger political pedigree.

I decided it was time to tell my company Chairman what I was up to. I told him that I wasn't looking to leave but the opportunity was there and I wanted to give it my best shot. He shared my assessment of the low likelihood of success but nevertheless was most supportive. Perhaps to steer me off the idea, he also promoted me to Group Managing Director.

My next move was to try and put down some markers throughout the region. Although I had roots throughout the West Midlands, I was unknown politically outside Stratford. As Stratford was only one of the 59 Westminster constituencies in the region, I had a lot of work to do. The easy bit was a flurry of letters to local papers on various vaguely European topics. They were published, but I knew I needed to do more than that. Fate took a hand when Philip Bradbourn lost his voice.

Phil was the West Midlands Regional Conservative Chairman, an unpaid volunteer, who was widely respected by party members throughout the region. The word was that he was going to stand for MEP. Alongside

Malcolm Harbour, who had already been a candidate at earlier European elections, Phil would probably be my biggest rival. He was due to speak at a Conservative Conference at the National Motor Cycle Museum near Birmingham, but his voice disappeared and so did he.

When the organiser, who I had met previously, asked me to fill in at short notice and talk about my experience of doing business in Europe. I jumped at the opportunity. It turned out that the audience included several local Conservative Constituency Chairmen (who would ultimately be on the selection committee for MEP candidates). Fortunately my speech and the Q & A session that followed went down well, though I did have to field a difficult question from one Philip Gretton, vice-chairman of Redditch Conservative Association. He was to bombard me with relentless Eurosceptic letters over the coming months, I guess to make sure that if I got to Brussels I wouldn't go native. He need not have worried.

Soon afterwards, the lists opened for the West Midlands region. To apply, every approved candidate had to complete a fresh CV form. My heart sank. The new form was very specific, and entirely geared to full-time politicians. There were huge spaces to fill in regarding my presumed past political career, but no room to put in anything else. My form was going to be very empty and my new career looked like being over before it had begun. I rang Rachel Dyche for a moan. I shall never know whether that helped or not, but a much fuller four-page form was shortly issued just to the West Midlands applicants. With great relief, I sent off the overflowingly-completed form to join the 76 other applications.

The selection committee decided to interview only two dozen candidates. More than 50 applications were discarded, including those from former MPs such as Winston Churchill, Nick Budgen and Norman Lamont. This stage was the biggest hurdle and I reckoned that if I could just get through it, I would have a fair chance if given the opportunity to stand up and speak for myself at a later stage. I learned later that I just squeezed through.

Next stop was the semi-final, held over two days at the aptly named

Margaret Thatcher House at Kidderminster. I was told that it was advisable for spouses to be present at the lunch. When I phoned to say that Angela had arranged to be in London that day to help our daughter choose a wedding dress I was told again that it was advisable for spouses to be present at the lunch....

So the wedding dress had to wait, and Angela went shopping instead for some power clothes for herself. I still think she was the real reason I got through this next stage as she was at her sparkling best. I was actually very nervous about this session, because the prize was getting so close.

I began very solemnly by saying that certain unsuccessful candidates had written to the press saying how badly the selectors had behaved by excluding them, then went on to say that I personally thought that the selectors had clearly done an excellent job. I added that I hoped to still be in a position to say the same when the weekend was over. They laughed happily.

The ice was broken, and the rest of the half-hour was no problem. The final questioner asked me to keep the answer short, but was I in favour of a federal Europe and did I support the UK joining the Single Currency. I replied "No", and asked if the answer was short enough. It was and I was through.

One last hurdle remained, the grand final at the National Exhibition Centre. It took place in May on the hottest day of the year. Some 230 party members spent the day listening to twelve candidates in succession, each talking for ten minutes and then answering questions for twenty. If it was daunting for us, it must have been dire for them.

The candidates met at 9am and drew lots for the speaking order. I drew the last slot, which meant there was time for me to go home and try to relax. Returning later in the afternoon suitably refreshed, I was gifted the opening line:

"Ladies and Gentlemen, the moment you have all been waiting for. I am the last candidate!"

My prepared speech was timed to last no more than nine minutes, as I didn't want to overrun. I had started to write it three weeks earlier, and had polished it several times a day ever since. I thought it was the best speech I had ever made – and probably ever will make. It needed to be, for I was up against some talented and well-known opposition.

Then came the questions, at random from the floor. The first came from Philip Gretton: "How much further should the UK go down the road to European integration? "I gave a feeble answer, saying it was difficult to be specific. He was not impressed, and neither was I. I had to do better with the other questions and fortunately did, with the final question again an unexpected gift:

"Do you have any experience of television or radio interviews, and dealing with journalists – and could you keep the answer short".

I said "Yes." And the audience laughed and applauded loudly, probably because their ordeal was over.

The count now began. The audience was asked to vote for between four and eight candidates, awarding eight points for first place preference, seven points for second and so on down to one point for eighth. Angela had chosen to come into the hall with me when my turn came in to speak, and leave with me when I finished. This meant she couldn't stay to vote so I lost eight votes in the process (always assuming, of course, that she would have voted for me). We both felt her presence with me would be worth more votes than the eight we lost. We would soon know.

I rushed back and forth, leaning over the various scrutineers, doing my own calculations. It was clear that John Corrie was in the lead with Malcolm Harbour and I fighting it out for second place. At last the candidates were then ushered into a private room to hear the results and be asked if they accepted the proffered place.

The final order was:
1) John Corrie   He accepted
2) Me   I did too

3) Malcolm Harbour	So did he
4) Sarah Biffen	She declined, saying a No. 4 slot couldn't win
5) Philip Bradbourn	He accepted the number 4 slot with disbelief and delight.

Our final five to eight were Richard Normington, Virginia Taylor, Mark Greenburgh and Michael Burnett, all of whom were to play a major part in the ensuing campaign.

Amazingly, as a political virgin, I had secured the coveted No 2 slot. Conservatives were certain to get at least three MEPs at the elections the following year. I would be one of them. Only eight months had elapsed since I had even first considered the idea, yet now I was guaranteed to become a Member of the European Parliament in 14 months' time. It was really quite extraordinary.

I should have realised that in politics nothing is guaranteed. I had reckoned without the House of Lords.

Chapter Two

A Famous Victory

Back at work on Monday I immediately called my Company Chairman to tell him I would be resigning next May. There was no way I could stay on as Managing Director and be an active MEP as well. Both were full-time jobs. I also gave notice to shed my Non-Exec Directorships: I had been a member of the 3i Independent Directors' Panel for several years, and leaving this was to be another wrench.

The European Parliamentary elections were fixed for June 1999, just over a year into the future. I was on an eighteen-month rolling contract with Red Mill, but thought that giving a full year's notice of my leaving would be okay. Secretly I hoped that I might be allowed to step down early the following Spring: the extra few months out and about in the region would certainly come in useful, since I had so much to learn.

The Press meanwhile were most interested in the West Midlands result as well as the results from other regions, particularly as the Conservatives were the first major party to complete their selection process. The *Daily Telegraph* ran a helpful guide to readers, which pigeon-holed each of the successful Conservative candidates. Alongside each name it put the label 'Europhile' or 'Eurosceptic'. Against my name, with no political pedigree available, it had to settle for the word 'businessman'.

The paper was also most interested in the different selection procedures being used by each of the three major parties. Although Conservatives despised this new list system, the party had to make the best job it could out of it and decided to leave the choice up to the members. Central Office had to approve the initial candidates, but this was not done on the basis of political rightness, leftness or correctness. They were looking for integrity, commitment, energy and the ability to communicate rather than a particular Eurosceptic/Europhile balance. After the initial 'approval', it was to be up to the grass roots membership to decide who they wanted once they had seen and heard the candidates for themselves. And the system worked – well, it certainly worked for me.

The Liberal Democrats devised a unique version of democracy in their selection process. They were keen to ensure they had a 'fair' number of female MEPs. So their central office decided to have <u>two</u> lists of eight per region, a male list and a female list. These were then to be 'zipped' together alternately by sex, with the top four male and female candidates producing the final list of eight. To make sure that females headed at least half the combined lists, alternate regions would be headed by alternate sexes. The LibDem powers-that-be determined that the East Midlands would be headed by a male even if the top female had more votes, and the West Midlands list would be headed by a female regardless of whether or not the top male had more votes. The LibDems always did try to be different.

In the West Midlands Liz Lynne, a former Westminster MP for Rochdale, topped the female list. Being the right sex she became the certainty to be an MEP the following year.

All LibDems loved the new system. It was Proportional Representation, which for them was by definition a Good Thing. It would give them a seat in most regions. In fact the approval of the Liberal Democrats was one of the reasons for the change to the new system in the first place. Tony Blair felt that in the mid-term of the Westminster Parliament Labour might be less popular, and strong LibDem support would keep votes from leaching to the Conservatives. By agreeing to proportional representation for the European Parliament, Blair could be seen to be honouring his pledge to move in this direction while simultaneously stalling on bringing in P.R. to the House of Commons. A cunning plan.

The PM also had another reason for changing the selection process. With the control-freakishness that was to become one of his trademarks, he wanted to oversee the selection of the candidates in detail from the centre. Above all, he wanted to oversee the de-selection of candidates. If he allowed the party members to decide, there was always the risk they might come up with the wrong answer.

In the West Midlands, some of the seven current Labour MEPs would not be available this next time round. Phillip Whitehead's constituency covered Burton-on-Trent in Staffordshire, as well as parts of Derbyshire, thereby straddling the new East and West Midlands regions. He decided to move East for re-selection. Christine Crawley and John Tomlinson, who had shared Birmingham, were being sent to the Lords. There were going to be at least some Labour vacancies.

The official Labour party machine clearly had views about two other sitting MEPs. Christine Oddy, in her second term as MEP for Coventry and North Warwickshire, had performed powerfully in Brussels, putting her stamp on several key pieces of legislation. She had also managed to be a very active constituency MEP, being especially visible in support of the disadvantaged. She was vigorous in pursuing the interests of pensioners, and was often to be seen in deprived areas of her constituency. However, the party apparatchiks wanted her seat for someone else and so although her constituents loved her, and strongly supported her re-nomination, Labour Central Office arbitrarily put her in at number seven on their list with no chance of success.

In Hereford and Shropshire, the Labour MEP was David Hallam. He had been the surprise victor five years previously in defeating the incumbent Conservative MEP Christopher Prout (who had the wonderfully appropriate nickname of Brusselsprout). Since then, although David had made comparatively little impact in the Parliament by comparison with Christine, he had made a substantial impact back in his constituency. He had embraced many local good causes, made regular contacts with local business and the farming community, and had built considerable cross-party support. He too was to be dumped, though not as drastically as Christine Oddy. He at least was allowed the number five slot, with Michael Tappin (MEP for Staffordshire) one ahead in the marginal number four position.

Simon Murphy was the sitting MEP for the Wolverhampton area, and he was sure to be re-nominated. Whatever the Labour leadership wanted, he was going to be right there, mouthing the right phrases. He had only ever been in politics and was a politician through and through. He also had a strong local base of support, which he had worked hard to achieve.

Labour had decided centrally that Simon was to be the number one – and within seven months of the election would for a short time become the Leader of the whole Labour MEP group. But into the number two and three slots Labour amazingly ignored all the local options and parachuted in two Londoners.

At number two was Michael Cashman, an active member of the Labour National Executive and an equally active Gay Rights campaigner. When he was asked what connection he had with the West Midlands, he said he had once acted in the Rocky Horror Show at the Birmingham Rep. Experience of rocky horror might indeed be useful background experience for dealing with Brussels bureaucracy. It did not however impress the local radio interviewer as a strong reason for representing the West Midlands. A colleague later saw his original application form, which said how much he was looking forward to representing London.

At number three, Labour Central Office equally thoughtfully selected Neena Gill, who ran a Housing association again in the London area. It was suspected by some that she had been picked because of her Asian background: West Midlands Asians were furious because of they felt it implied that none of the local Asians were any good. Both became clearly badged as Tony's cronies.

Local Labour party activists from the east and west of the region were apoplectic with rage, saying the fact that Christine and David had been dumped was a 'defeat for democracy', and said they wouldn't work for the Labour list. Christine Oddy talked publicly about her "anger at Labour betrayal", and was soon threatening to take Labour to an Industrial Tribunal with a claim for unfair dismissal. She was to be dropped from the list altogether. David Hallam grinned and bore it, still clinging to the slim hope that he might squeak back as an MEP if Labour were to win five out of the eight seats: when that failed to happen in the election the following June, he too let rip.

This was one of the major mistakes of the Labour campaign. The people wanted to choose their own candidates, but Labour was no longer listening.

Meanwhile, other regions had yet to complete their selection of Conservative candidates. On learning of my result a fellow businessman from the East Midlands, Roger Helmer, rang up to ask what was the secret of success. A fellow groupie from my selection board, Theresa Villiers, rang with the same question. I advised them both: don't be defensive about your lack of a political record but play it as a strength, and don't use a single note when you speak. Both of them promptly came top of their respective lists. Although I would like to take total credit for their achievement, I suspect the fact they were extremely strong candidates had something to do with the result. Roger would soon earn a reputation as the most vigorous of fighters against a federal Europe; inside three years Theresa would be elected deputy Leader of the Conservative MEP delegation.

Back in the West Midlands the Conservative team had already started to plan for the future, and began a series of bi-monthly meetings at weekends to shape our programme and priorities for the coming year. Our target was four seats: three should be secure but we all wanted to get Phil Bradbourn elected alongside the top three. I felt that we should divide the region into four quarters, with each becoming the responsibility of one of the 'first' four candidates, who would then be paired with one of the second four. John Corrie was the sitting MEP for Worcestershire and South Warwickshire but living in Worcestershire, while I was the sitting candidate living in Warwickshire. I suggested to John that he should match Hereford with his home county of Worcestershire: they were already linked in a joint Chamber of Commerce. In turn, I might link Warwickshire with Shropshire. He agreed readily, and was happy to propose this at our first meeting. Coming from John it was accepted as a splendid idea, and it formed the basis of our approach in the months to come.

Paired with me was Virginia Taylor, who was shortly moving to the Hereford area anyway. She had great ideas, energy and vitality, and despite having an important job to complete in London was always in the constituency whenever she was needed.

Or perhaps I should say soon after she was needed. Until her house move was completed, her hectic life meant that she was always trying to be in several places at once. For most events she was never quite on time: it was her own idea to call herself 'the late Mrs Taylor.'

Richard, Mark and Michael were also towers of strength. Even though they had no chance of being elected this time around they worked their butts off in the cause. Each of them still cherished hopes of a political career in due course, and each deserves it mightily.

Each of the 'first' four evolved naturally into differing roles. John, as our one existing MEP, led on political issues. I developed contacts in the media, the food industry and the business community in general. Malcolm joined me in developing business contacts and drew on his immense experience in the motor trade – he had been a director of Rover in earlier times and was now a partner in his own international car trade consultancy. He was also our TechnoWizard, the master of the computer and the web-site, who developed an audio-visual programme, unravelling the complexities of the new voting system, which became widely admired nationally throughout the party. As a Euro-candidate on two previous occasions, he also knew the ropes about campaigning. Phil Bradbourn handled the local government side: for many years he had been the professional adviser to the Conservative Group leader on Wolverhampton Borough Council. He knew everything there was to know about local government and a whole lot more.

Our activities were co-ordinated by a master schedule, run with extreme efficiency and impartiality by Malcolm's wife Penny; this helped us to ensure that we didn't overlap, and that we all knew what each of us were doing and where we were doing it.

Our mission in the second half of that year was really just to talk to Conservatives. The task was not going to be to persuade non-supporters to vote Conservative: it was to persuade Conservatives to come out and vote. So we had to go out far and wide, in evenings and at weekends, to fire up the faithful.

In virtually all constituencies we were made most welcome, and the members and supporters couldn't wait to invite us back. Only two constituencies I recall were slightly harder work, at least initially.

One was Aldridge Brownhills, base of Richard Shepherd MP. Richard was known to be one of the champions of Westminster Parliamentary democracy, and for him the forces at loose in the corridors of Brussels were dark and sinister. I got the feeling he would be much happier if the European Parliament did not exist. At times, I thought he felt the same about the European Union too.

The other was Ludlow, the kingdom of Christopher Gill. As another 'Maastricht rebel', he too had very clear views on Europe, and had been the only MP to turn up at our final selection meeting at the NEC. I dared to go into the lion's den soon afterwards, and got myself invited to the Ludlow Conservative Association Annual Dinner. I hadn't met Christopher until that evening, and arrived early to meet as many individual members as possible before we all sat down at table. Christopher made no move to approach me, until I received a sudden summons from the Association Chairman that "Mr Gill would like to see you at the top of the stairs". I felt like a naughty schoolboy being called before the head-teacher.

Christopher said he had been very concerned at some of the points I had made in my NEC speech. I had dared to utter the phrases "Pro-European" and "We should all be positive Europeans now", though both phrases were used by William Hague. Christopher added that however I had just about redeemed myself by being the only candidate who had mentioned the key word 'freedom'. I felt I might perhaps have edged myself onto his Christmas card list after all, but that we were unlikely to be great kindred spirits.

I could not have been more wrong. Christopher was to be hugely supportive throughout the campaign. Much as he was unhappy with the European Parliament, he was realist enough to know that it was there, it was going to stay there, and it was better to fill it with active Conservative MEPs than with more of the socialist lot who were running the place at that moment.

Christopher and I subsequently spoke on various platforms together, met at Local Authority meetings, and he introduced me around at the Shropshire and WestMid Agricultural Show. He knew everybody, and was widely respected both as a good constituency MP, and as one who stood up fearlessly for what he believed in. I was grateful for his support, and was delighted to give him mine.

Over the coming months I was to meet two other Tory heavyweights. The first was Christopher Prout, now Lord Kingsland. He gave me some deep background on the constituency, as well as his perspective of the European Parliament. He had been Leader of the Conservative MEPs for many years, and it was a privilege to share his insight. His secretary also gave me some wise advice: don't kill yourself time-wise during the campaign – it wasn't worth it. This was sound advice indeed, though increasingly difficult to keep once the campaign took off.

The other heavyweight was William Hague. I had first met him when he visited the Midlands on his campaign to become Leader. He spoke with a force and energy that reminded me of Margaret Thatcher, and with an equal passion for the Conservative cause. He was also immensely entertaining. When a variety of questions were flung at him afterwards he actually answered them, and did so with brevity, clarity and wit. He was clearly pitching for local support for his candidacy, and certainly earned it on that day.

An enduring memory of that occasion was the question asked by my fellow Harbury villager (and successor as local Branch Chairman) Sheila Allan. She asked if William agreed that although it was a serious business working for the party, shouldn't we all try and make it more fun at the same time? William, and the audience, agreed heartily. At the end of the session there was a long list of names supporting William Hague. Had there been one, the list for those who wanted to have fun with Sheila Allan would have been even longer.

I met William several more times during the year, in the region, at conferences and on the campaign trail. He seemed to have all the qualities needed for a really strong leader except one: he just didn't come across well on television. So many people commented that if only everybody could actually meet the man it would be no contest between him and Blair. Irritatingly Blair's mastery of the media still kept him well ahead in the opinion polls at least for the time being.

But even William was very out of favour with the candidates for several months during the autumn of 1998. Although all the parties had completed their selection process on the basis of the new PR system, it now transpired that Tony Blair had omitted to sign off the legislation. The Lords had a chance to throw it out, and prompted by the Tory leadership that's what they did.

There clearly was a genuine issue of principle at stake: the party list system of candidates sharing mega-constituencies was widely perceived to be undemocratic, and the Conservatives had denounced it at the start. Now there was a real chance for the Tories – in the Commons and the Lords – to stand up for democracy. The Lords were in especially stroppy mood at that time because the hereditary peers were about to be junked, and this was their final chance to flex their muscles. But the principle was the issue, and the draft legislation bounced back and forth between Lords and Commons not once but six times.

Labour threatened to give in and re-instate the first-past-the-post system, expecting the Tory bluff to be called (Conservatives thought they stood to gain more seats under the new PR system). But William stood his ground, and the Lords would not be moved.

Now this showdown may have played well at Westminster, with the two parties scoring points off each other in the two Chambers, but it didn't play at all in the real world. People I talked to were either unaware of the debate, or just didn't see it as one of the burning issues facing the nation. The feeling was that it was just another example of politicians playing games with other politicians, while the real battle for the people's hearts and minds was not engaged.

While it didn't play at all for the public, it played extremely badly for the candidates. Indeed were we even candidates any more? Would there have to be a completely new selection process, on the old constituency boundaries?

Roger Helmer rang me in turmoil asking what our leadership was playing at, and what should he do? I advised him to do what I was doing, and help jam Party Chairman Michael Ancram's fax machine. I gave him the number.

It was already jammed.

Both Roger and I had resigned our jobs and given up our business careers. He had already left. In my case, as my letter of resignation had never been formally acknowledged, I wrote again and withdrew it. This completely threw my Chairman, who was well into final interviews with possible successors. By December, the Chairman was ready to make an offer to the new M.D. He had discussed my situation with the company's lawyers, who had never come across a situation quite like it. They were committed to replace someone who they didn't want to lose and who didn't want to go, but if they failed to replace him he might go anyway and leave the position unfilled for months. Their solution was that they made me a generous offer, so I agreed in December that I would leave at the end of February regardless. I burned my boats and held my breath.

By now there was beginning to be a degree of nudging and winking from Central Office that the point had been made, and that Tony Blair would invoke the Parliament Act and ensure that the will of the Commons prevailed. He had been unable to do that originally because clumsily he had allowed the original bill to start life in the Lords rather than the Commons. Under arcane Parliamentary procedure that meant he had to wait for a year and a day after its introduction, and for a new

Parliamentary session (which had just begun in November) before he could trigger that process. He did so reluctantly, and the candidates could breathe again.

Tory Lords and MPs were cock-a-hoop at the embarrassment that they had caused the Government. The media, the membership, and above all the candidates all thought they were potty.

That hiccup behind us, the weeks then flashed by until suddenly we were in full campaign mode. Malcolm had managed to get hold of four Rover Discoveries, and had got them all dolled up with Conservative logos together with the magic message 'In Europe, not run by Europe'. We were told to repeat this phrase ourselves relentlessly in every speech on as many occasions as possible, and we did. By the time that Election Day dawned I was to become heartily sick of hearing that constant refrain. But it had powerful appeal, and it was to win us the election. Research had shown that 77% of all voters agreed with it, and an amazing 79% of Labour voters agreed with it too. Certainly, whenever I was campaigning and people were struggling to put into words what they felt about Europe, once I mentioned our special slogan their eyes lit up and they said: Exactly right!

It was a great message.

Our other message concerned the Single Currency. It was the one issue that everyone wanted to talk about. 'What was my view on joining the Single Currency?' though all too often this was confusingly expressed as 'Should we go into Europe?' (meaning into the Euro). Initially I chose to duck the question, saying that it was nothing to do with Brussels or indeed MEPs. This would be decided in Westminster after a referendum in which they would all have a chance to vote. The Euro was not an issue for this election.

But in the eyes of many of the electorate it was indeed an issue. For most it was the only issue.

When I had originally ducked the question people assumed that I was reluctant to give an answer and were clearly not impressed. So I started to answer the question, and said No. For them, it was the right answer.

We were still worried though as to whether our overall message was getting across. Labour had decided to play a very low-key campaign, and generally tried to avoid talking about Europe at all. They didn't even have a separate manifesto for the election: they just trotted out the manifesto for the Party of European Socialists (PES), which was not exactly a turn-on for the UK. Their local message seemed to be: save our schools and the NHS and keep the Tories out. Also, because they appeared to be deliberately avoiding issuing European Press releases and turning down media interviews, we were often told as Conservative candidates: "Sorry, we cannot run your story because we can't get a comment from the other side, and we have to keep a balance".

This was very clever media manipulation by Labour. It made the final election outcome that much juicier because it backfired.

In early May, Central Office suddenly sent us all pagers. At last we were, literally, to be on the same wavelength as MPs. We were going to be on message. Actually, they ended up as an anti-climax. The messages from on high usually only arrived at mid-day. To be interrupted in mid-speech to local farmers by a vibrating gadget pronouncing proudly that the theme of the day was tax harmonisation did not seem particularly designed to help win over extra votes on the ground.

Various highlights from the campaign are worth recounting. There was the trip to Harborne in Birmingham, where I was accosted by a lady who asked if I agreed with her about a key priority for Europe. There needed to be more toilets in Harborne High Street. Anxious for her vote, I feebly agreed: somehow this priority never made it to the manifesto.

We were all out on the streets so much it didn't seem necessary to hold public meetings, but I decided to hold one in my home village of Harbury. It would be an open discussion on all matters European, and everyone was welcome. We booked the local school, and publicised the event well in advance throughout the neighbouring villages. I knew we would have at least six people – the local Branch Committee had no choice in the matter. Come the day, and fearful that we might only have the six, I dragooned my local builder into coming along too. We were now sure of seven, who were to be sprinkled widely throughout the hall to give an illusion of numbers.

In the end the final tally was eight: the unexpected extra was a potential UK Independence Party (UKIP) voter from Worcester. The meeting consisted of a dialogue between Worcester-man and me, and at the end I felt the result was at best a draw. Afterwards he rang to say he would be voting with us after all, but it was not I who had convinced him. When he had begun to speak he had said that he was a stranger - to which our new Branch Chairman had responded that nobody was a stranger in the Conservative Party. His opposition melted. Sheila Allan had struck again.

Every morning, noon and night all eight of us were somewhere in the region, walking the streets, speaking to local groups, or accosting people in shopping centres. In between we would be driving around in the Discoveries booming out through the specially installed sound system: "Vote Conservative. Your local Conservative candidate, John/Philip/ Malcolm/Phil, is in such-and-such a place today. Only the Conservatives want to be in Europe, not run by Europe." Once when Virginia Taylor was on the mike, out came a rather different message: "Only the Conservatives want to be in Europe, not part of Europe". I am not sure whether in that town we won more votes or less.

In Burton-on-Trent I was canvassing outside the local Sainsbury's one day, aided and abetted by my friend Derek Markham. The manager came out after a while to say that a complaint had been made that I was harassing all the customers on the way in. (This was not true - I was harassing them on the way out.) This at least made a change from another complaint: Phil Bradbourn later reported that when he chanted "Save the Pound" outside a certain supermarket, several shoppers had asked which special offer he was on about.

Anyway, when the manager saw I was a candidate he immediately apologised for having to pass on what was clearly a phoney complaint: the opposition was clearly just trying to make life difficult. On his advice I moved three feet further away, no longer on Sainsbury property, and therefore beyond his and the customers' jurisdiction.

Not everyone in Burton was so keen to speak to me. On several occasions people were complaining to Derek that they never saw a real candidate. Once he pointed out that there was a very real one just yards away they always turned and fled.

I was surprised how much I enjoyed being on the stump, and also how little I was missing business that had been my life for the previous thirty odd years. Food manufacturing seemed a lifetime away. I hoped that I would not get so caught up in the thrill of the campaign that I would forget why I had put my name forward in the first place.

Certainly the campaign seemed to be going very well. The defining moment was in the streets of Worcester with a couple of weeks to go. People came up to me saying that they were lifelong Labour (or LibDem) supporters, but this time around they would be voting Conservative for the first time ever because of our policies on Europe. They wanted to be in Europe, but not run by Europe. They had got the message. We were heading for a famous victory.

Election Day came, and the votes were 'verified' later that evening. That meant the ballot papers were counted (face down, but we could often see through), the totals confirmed, and put in secure boxes. The count proper would take place at the National Indoor Arena on Sunday 13th June, in order to co-ordinate with the count across the EU on the same day.

The count itself was an anticlimax, because we were so certain of the result. The electors of Worcester had already confirmed it for us weeks before. When the final outcome was announced in the early hours, we were too tired to raise much of a cheer. We had been on the stump for over twelve months. But we had got our four seats with votes to spare.

The week before the election, the Conservatives were some minus 23% in the polls. The week after, we were still some 23% behind. But in the week in the middle, in the one poll that mattered, we were 8% ahead. The rout of Labour was echoed throughout the country, with our national tally more than doubling to 36 MEPs and Labour more than halving to 29.

We would like to believe that the West Midlands success of going from one MEP to four was of course entirely due to the particular merits of the candidates. We were soon to be disabused.

The *Hereford Times* announced the successful Conservatives by first names only, proudly presenting us as John Alexander, Philip Rodway, Malcolm Charles and Philip Charles. Obviously we had made our mark in Hereford.

The *Worcester Evening News* referred to me as a biscuit manufacturer from Birmingham, and Malcolm as running his own car spare-parts business in Solihull. We had clearly gone down well in Worcester too.

And a local journalist rang anxious to speak to Mr Obe. He refused to be put off, saying he wanted to talk to our fourth successful candidate. It was only then that we recalled that Phil Bradbourn was an Officer of the Order of the British Empire. His name was recorded as Philip Bradbourn OBE.

The following day we realised that the campaign must be over. Just when we had become real MEPs rather than candidates, just when the media were at last interested to hear our views on all the political issues of the moment, Central Office considerately switched off our pagers.

Chapter Three

Three weeks on, three weeks off

I was now an MEP. For the first time in my life I had a five-year contract – and for a job for which I had no training and no previous experience. It was all rather odd.

What I found even odder was to be told that although I was legally an MEP with immediate effect, I wouldn't be paid for seven weeks until the end of the following month. Even odder, I couldn't yet go to the Parliament.

However, on the first week of July the new crop of MEPs were going to be allowed to meet somewhere else, to ease their way gently into the job by getting together in their political groupings. Our Group briefing session was to be in Marbella. Well, it had to be somewhere, and Marbella was cheaper than Brussels.

The political grouping we were to be allied with was called the EPP. This was a centre-right grouping of parties from all 15 Member States.

There were to be 233 MEPs in this Group now, up from 200 the time before as a direct result of the swing to the right across Europe. The UK Conservatives made up a significant 36 of the total. We were a varied bunch. There were some former MEPs and former MPs. There were two Lords, one Earl, and a Knight of the Realm. There were Eurosceptics and Europhiles – and the great news for me that there were also other businessmen. We had a common mission, and together felt confident we could deliver.

Back in the UK there had been a lot of argument about whether we should throw in our lot with the EPP or not. They were seen by many at home as a Federalist party, pushing for further European integration, and this did not square with our "In Europe not run by Europe" mantra.

The Conservatives, thanks to William Hague, Shadow Foreign Secretary John Maples and Edward McMillan Scott, had negotiated a clever deal that made our arrangement very flexible. We were to become associate members only. This meant we were not committed to any EPP Group manifesto: we were only bound by our own. On issues such as European integration, tax harmonisation, the single currency etc., it was acknowledged we would vote very differently from the rest of the Group. The Group would also change its name to accommodate us.

Our original idea was to get the word 'Conservative' into the title. Unfortunately that word had negative connotations in some languages and to some nationalities, especially the Germans. So the new name was agreed to be the Group of the European Peoples' Party/European Democrats, or EPP/ED for short (in French of course it had to be PPE/DE). It didn't exactly trip off the tongue, but it did signal change.

Certain fellow UK MEPs were still uneasy about even this loose alliance, given the perceived federalist aura. Because prominent members of this group included Roger Helmer, Daniel Hannan and Chris Heaton-Harris, they became known as the H-Block.

The H-Block had proposed a separate, purist identity, even though this would have given us little leverage in the Parliament to promote our manifesto commitments. As it was, we had the best of both worlds.

The benefits of this new arrangement would become vividly clear in 2001. Tony Blair had refused to hold a Public Inquiry into the lessons to be learnt from the Foot and Mouth epidemic. He had good reason to fear what such an Inquiry might reveal. Conservative MEP Robert Sturdy conceived the idea of invoking a rarely used EU procedure. This involved calling for a Temporary Committee to be set up to hold a Public Inquiry at EU level. One quarter of all the MEPs would be needed to support such a procedure, and the advantages of kinship with a large group rapidly became clear when all the EPP/ED weighed in behind his proposal.

The Socialists tried to vote the proposal down, but were hopelessly outnumbered.

William himself came out to join us in Marbella, and confirm the position in what became known as 'The Malaga Declaration', cannily called after the name of the region rather than the town. 'The Marbella Declaration' would have sounded too much as if we were on a jolly. He confirmed that there was a wide diversity of views within the new EPP/ED Group, and went on to explain why. Right wing parties are by definition different from each other: believing in freedom and democracy, such parties are shaped by local/regional/national identities and institutions. Socialists in contrast tended to vote in a solid brotherly block. We had to ensure that we were collectively strong enough to defeat them, and that we used this strength to deliver our manifesto.

The meeting on day one was my first experience of simultaneous translation, which was to become a regular feature of my new life. Around the room were eleven booths, with three interpreters in each, for each of the eleven official languages in the Parliament. The threesome would rotate 5–10 minute stints between each of them, translating the words of the various speakers just half a sentence later. This was a special challenge for those trying to translate out of German: they had to wait until the end of the sentence to hear the verb before they could understand what the speaker meant, and then had to rush to catch up. It must have been tiring work.

We all sat with headphones on – except for those multi-lingual members who conspicuously left theirs off to show that they understood what was being said irrespective of the language. But there was always a general scramble for the headphones whenever the Danes or the Finns started to speak.

Briefing papers were available on the way in, in all languages of course. A band of a different colour distinguished each language version. I don't know who had decided and when, but I was advised that throughout the EU institutions 'English is pink'.

It was altogether a most stimulating week, meeting and listening to so many very bright people. Each national delegation detailed its election successes and their views on the key issues for the future. All had one message in common: for the first time ever in the European Parliament, the Centre-Right grouping of MEPs was ahead of the Socialists. At long last we were in a position to lead, and we were all determined to use this strength to drive change.

One of the changes which I was to hear much more of in the coming months was that Parliament had to start showing its teeth. Too often, the formerly Socialist-led Parliament had just rubber-stamped Socialist-led legislation from the Socialist-led Commission. Much change was clearly needed. We went home invigorated by the debates, and looking forward to the future: the following week we were actually being allowed a brief visit to Brussels!

After a hectic round of constituency engagements at the weekend, Angela and I drove to Belgium on the Sunday evening together with son William. While I went to the Parliament, they would scout around for a flat to rent. The car was filled with spare suits, shirts etc, so that I would be all set up at the earliest opportunity.

The first challenge on arrival in the deserted city centre at 10pm on Sunday night was to find the official parliament car park. John Corrie had kindly loaned me his special MEP swipe card, as I wouldn't get my own until I had officially been signed in. I had also been given helpful instructions on where the car park was. It was just off the Rue Belliard and impossible to miss.

It was indeed well signposted. We saw the first sign easily, advising us the turn-off was 100 metres further on. Then we saw the actual entrance, below another large sign. The booth was unmanned and the entrance barrier was down, but this was understandable given that it was late on Sunday night.

I drove down the ramp under the automatic barrier, which obligingly lifted and came down behind us. We then turned a corner to be confronted by a rusting door, partly off its hinges, which clearly signified a very old entrance to an equally old car park. The gate wouldn't open. When we reversed, neither would the automatic barrier.

I was not going to be defeated by my first challenge in Brussels. With the help of my six-foot son, the two of us just managed to bend (literally) the barrier upwards sufficiently for Angela to reverse the car under and out. There the car stayed, its rear overhanging the Rue Belliard, while I walked the 800 metres to the Parliament reception to ask where they had hidden the car park. Needless to say there was completely new car park (with no signs) around the corner. The old car park, complete with signs, had not been used for some while. It was an early lesson in the Parliament's poor communication skills. It would be fully twelve months before these signs were removed.

The following morning I presented myself at the Parliament afresh, trying to look nothing like the dishevelled creature who had called the night before. I was formally photographed, and given a temporary pass while the proper one was prepared. As an afterthought I asked whether I could sign in Angela and William for the day, to be told to my amazement that spouses and student children could obtain a full five-year pass to all the facilities in the Parliament. We were the first in the queue.

The next hour was taken up filling in the various forms necessary to open a bank account. Two further visits to the bank would be required before I was formally up and running. Bureaucracy was clearly alive and well in Brussels.

I thought it would be a good idea to find my office, and may be even get into it. The office dispensing the keys would open at 10.30am, so I was there at around 10.15 so as not to lose any time. There was already a queue. The door indeed opened at 10.30. I got my key an hour later.

There were three people helping. The first one wrote down the MEP's name on a piece of paper and passed it to the second. The second disappeared for a while to look up in a ledger the number appropriate to the MEP, and wrote that down on a different piece of paper. This was then handed to a third person who vanished for a while to reappear triumphantly in due course with one key (to be signed for in triplicate). As I was amongst the first, I was one of the lucky ones. Those behind me, now in a long queue stretching round many corners, became more and more fraught, especially when they heard the announcement that at 12.30 the office would close for the normal two-hour lunch. The desk was promptly stormed by the MEPs at the front, who refused to let the officials lock up or leave. The office didn't close that day. The MEPs had won, in a clear signal that the new crop were not the same as the old ones. We meant business.

With great glee I went up to my office. It was a double office, half for me and half for my non-existent assistant. It had a splendid view. It also had a private shower, basin and toilet, plus a TV with around 60 channels in various languages. This was luxury indeed. I decided to 'phone a friend' to celebrate, but the phone would not respond. To unlock it I needed a special code. That meant a visit to another office.

I also needed to get a car-park pass. Another office. I needed a Belgian ID Card: another office. I needed a Rail Card, to get free rail travel in Belgium and Luxembourg: another office. I also needed a special *Laisser-Passer* for use at the airport: yet another office. The first visit of course would be just to sign the forms: I would later have to return for another round of visits to collect and sign for the respective cards. I began to realise why the Parliament did not start straight away: at this rate it would be weeks before new MEPs had any spare time available for work.

A quick word about the *Laisser-Passer*. It was only useable at Brussels International airport, and it acted like a magic wand. You could bypass passport control, on entry and exit, just by flashing it at the official who was checking everyone else. A button would be pressed and a special door, reserved for staff but usable also by MEPs, would open just for us. This was to save a huge amount of time, week in and week out, and I am sure bemused other passengers who must have wondered how they could get such a card for themselves.

In the early afternoon of the first day, John Corrie led the three new

West Midlands MEPs on a brisk walk along various roads near the Parliament so that we could get our bearings. Angela and Penny Harbour came along too so that they could suss out the flat rental opportunities. Then while the girls carried on sussing we went back to the Parliament for a Group meeting.

This meeting, and the others that followed it over the next few days, were unlike any meetings I had ever attended. For example, having elected our new Group leader, Hans-Gert Pöttering from Germany, it was clear that the role of the Chairman was a delicate one. As there were thirty different parties represented, each with their own leaders, the Chairman was not absolutely the boss as such. He could only operate at any time by agreement. At each meeting, he did not determine the agenda but could only propose it. Anyone who wanted to speak had the right to speak. I had visions of very long meetings.

This was confirmed when there were six nominations for the six posts of Vice-Presidents (deals having been done back-stage). One might have thought that with six candidates for six vacancies it would be a relatively quick affair. Not so. This was Brussels. Speaker after speaker got up to say how good one particular candidate or another was - all extremely fascinating, but somewhat irrelevant as they were all going to get the job. I later learned that the number of votes for each candidate did in fact matter, as the rank order of the six would determine their relative roles.

One day the UK Conservatives had a meeting with Sir Stephen Wall, the UK Ambassador to the EU: to my surprise he was but one of our three Ambassadors in Brussels. Like other Member States, we also had our very own Ambassador to the Court of the King of the Belgians, and an Ambassador to NATO. Brussels must be the most over-ambassadored city in the world.

Although the meeting was to meet Sir Stephen, he brought along what he called his 'football team' of eleven followers. As they all trooped in a long line I must confess we all started laughing. What on earth did they all do, we wondered? Each took it in turns to explain their individual roles, but we were left none the wiser.

Another meeting with a difference was with the Parliament's own Secretariat, which was a Question and Answer session specifically for our EPP/ED Group. The UK Conservatives asked a mass of questions about policy, about procedures, and about the forthcoming hearings of the prospective Commissioners, and it was a very productive session. Afterwards we heard that it was in stark contrast to the earlier equivalent session with the Socialists. Their questions had mainly been about expense allowances.

As the largest Group, the EPP/ED had now commandeered the largest meeting room as ours by right for all our future meetings. A few Old Socialists occasionally wistfully put their head around the door, as it had always been their room until now. But times had changed. On the third day, Hans-Gert proudly announced the ultimate triumph: the name of our Group would be printed above the Party of European Socialists on all future lists of the various Group meetings. We were now, in every sense, on top. It was also reassuring to know that the key issue facing the future of Europe had been dealt with so promptly.

In between meetings and form-signings I made it my business to explore the whole building thoroughly. One of the first places I had to find was the Cash office, where I had to report each week to claim the daily allowances for living expenses. This was a system put in place some years previously apparently because some MEPs hardly ever turned up. A proportion of their 'income' was therefore made dependent upon being in the Parliament, where you had to sign in personally every day in order to prove you were there.

On Fridays, when MEPs left early to go home, this gave rise to the phrase Si-So. This stood for Sign in and Sod off.

My office was on the eighth floor of one block, with six lifts servicing it. There was never any wait. The key floor was the third, which was wide and open and linked by a passageway called the 'passarelle' to a second building where the hemicycle was. The hemicycle was the large chamber used for the full parliamentary sessions, and had room for all 626 MEPs.

I found the main restaurant, the members' restaurant and bar, and the library where all the daily newspapers were. I found the main coffee bar with its brightly coloured round and chubby furniture; I subsequently learnt that the Germans called it the Smarties Bar: we called it Play School. I found all the various committee meeting rooms, and the easiest way to get there. I also found someone to act as my assistant, Kelly Cumming, who had worked previously for Labour MEP Mike Tappin and therefore knew the West Midlands and the Parliament inside out. She was an immediate asset, and it was a great loss when a family tragedy impelled her to return home suddenly after only a few months. I was to be fortunate in rapidly finding a bubbly Belgian, Anne-Françoise Dethier, to take over in the run-up to Christmas.

Meanwhile, Angela had found a flat. It was bright and airy and looked over a park with the Parliament just beyond. It would take just five minutes to walk to the office. It was expensive, but just right.

She had also found it on her own, with minimal help from the Parliament staff. We had innocently expected that there might be some office somewhere whose mission it was to help new MEPs find accommodation. No chance. The officials were far too busy to help MEPs. Who on earth did MEPs think they were, anyway?

It had been a good week. I had (nearly) got all the right cards, though I didn't actually have any quite yet. I had (nearly) opened a bank account. I had actually got the key to the office door. I knew my way around the building. I had a research assistant. And I had a flat within walking distance. I was all set. Next week would be a new challenge: I would be off to Strasbourg.

Strasbourg is the official seat of the Parliament and where the main parliamentary votes take place for twelve sessions a year. It is ridiculous that we have to meet there as well as Brussels, but currently MEPs have no choice in the matter. The European Parliament is the only Parliament in the world that is not allowed to decide for itself where it sits. The Governments of the Member States have kindly decided that for us.

Brussels is the main centre, where we meet three weeks out of four. It is easy to get to. Three different airlines fly direct from Birmingham International Airport – or did in 1999. It is also the main home of the twenty EU Commissioners and their staff.

But once a month everyone ups sticks and goes to Strasbourg. It is a provincial city, rather than an international hub, so it is awkward to get to. MEPs from some countries have to leave their home on Sunday in order to arrive there by Monday afternoon. But it's not just MEPs who have to go there. So do the Commissioners and their staff, the interpreters, and all the administrators needed to run the place. Altogether nearly 3,000 people are coming and going each month. As well as the people, crates of documents go back and forth, and the post to each office in Brussels is diverted to Strasbourg every day.

The total on-cost of this to-ing and fro-ing is some £80 million a year, for the privilege of being in Strasbourg for just 48 days. The rest of the time the building is empty. Not only is it a huge waste of money, it is very inefficient. It is also literally unhealthy. Legionella thrives on stagnant water in dormant air-conditioning units. Because the water in the building doesn't move for 300 days a year there have been several occasions when the bug has been found and the building has had to be completely disinfected. Some of us have tried to use this as another argument to close the whole place down.

The reason we are there at all is because France, as a matter of national pride, insisted that the Parliament should meet in France. Strasbourg was chosen to represent reconciliation between the French and the Germans, who had fought over the city many times over the centuries. Designed to represent the future, this decision effectively represents the past. It also represents French intransigence, as they threatened to block all future legislation until the EU agreed.

Ironically this formal agreement at Council of Minister level was originally agreed by John Major at the Edinburgh Council meeting, on a five-year trial basis. He accepted this in part exchange for French approval that the UK could opt-out from the Social Chapter. On that basis it was a good deal. It was finally signed off as a permanent arrangement by Tony Blair and other EU leaders at the Treaty of Amsterdam, by which time Tony had signed up to the Social Chapter after all in exchange for nothing. On that basis it was a lousy deal, especially as it now needs unanimity amongst all Member States to unscramble the decision.

I later learned that before the decision was finalised in the Treaty, female MEPs used to get fresh flowers in their offices every day they were in Strasbourg. It was all part of the softening up process to get them on side. If any MEP ever spoke out in plenary complaining about anything Strasbourgish, or should I say Strasbourgeois, then some chocolates arrived too. However, once the position of Strasbourg was formally ratified, the wooing stopped. So did the flowers and the chocolates.

Meanwhile, as long as France holds onto its national veto, nothing will change. Given that we are adamant in the UK that we should keep our own national veto on matters of major national concern, we cannot in all fairness complain when other countries feel the same way. This is not an argument for surrendering the veto, merely an observation – but it is most frustrating.

To celebrate, the French constructed a futuristic new parliament building in Strasbourg, alongside the original one, at a cost to the French taxpayer of £350 million. The deal though was that the Parliament would reimburse the cost.

It is difficult to fly direct to Strasbourg from the West Midlands - or indeed from anywhere else in the EU for that matter. There is an Air France flight from Gatwick, but there was no way I was driving from the West Midlands all the way to Gatwick at dawn. Alternatively I could try Ryanair from Stansted. That had no appeal either.

Supporting my local airport Birmingham International instead, I was up early the following Monday to catch the first flight to Frankfurt, where I was met by a taxi to take me the rest of the way. On arrival, I discovered that David Hallam had been on the same plane. He was going to Strasbourg to collect his medal. Yes, departing MEPs do get a medal.

Now that the election was over he was very open with his thoughts on the way he had been treated. He had every right to feel he had been stitched up.

The centrepiece of the new Parliament is a wide hollow tower, with a vast empty courtyard in the middle. The building itself is entered via a single narrow escalator. So much space has been wasted on the courtyard there is not enough room inside.

The offices are a joke. There is still an individual shower, basin and toilet, as the French clearly consider that personal hygiene should take precedence over work facilities. There is no room for a filing cabinet. The printer has to be perched on top of the computer-stand so that my assistant has to get on a chair to reach it. Or she would if there was any room for an assistant: there is barely space for anyone else in the office.

I later learned that we could not just blame the French for this. The original plan was that the Tower would be for Commission staff, with MEPs remaining in their older but larger offices over the river bridge. But a Committee of MEPs had changed this after the design had essentially been finalised. Birmingham Labour MEP John Tomlinson had allegedly said that the Tower offices were the newest, and the nearest to the hemicycle, so they should be allocated to MEPs. As MEPs needed full bathroom facilities (and apparently staff didn't) what had been reasonable size offices in the plan became halved in size when loos and showers had to be retro-fitted. Order, Counter-Order, Disorder. I might have guessed that UK Labour MEPs would have got in the way somewhere along the line and screwed things up.

The signage around the building is so stylised as to be unintelligible: a completely new set had to be sellotaped to the wall at every junction before we returned in the autumn. On one corridor, a new sign was put up saying 'Bridge', with an arrow to the left. Underneath, someone had soon hand-written another sign saying 'Poker' with an arrow to the right.

To get to some of the committee rooms you have to descend from your office in the tower, find a connecting tunnel to the main block, and then queue up for one of the four tiny lifts to take you up the other side. You can try and use the stairs, but they miss out alternate floors and usually bypass the floor you want. The main lifts themselves are black inside following the insistence of the architect. After six months half at least had been lightened, at the insistence of MEPs. All the lifts are very slow and often stop at each floor: it takes so long to get anywhere that you either have to leave your office early or arrive at the meeting late. Usually it's both. Lord Stockton in a rare idle moment calculated that on average the lifts took two minutes to arrive. Used in general about ten times a day for four days during the twelve plenary sessions meant that MEPs spent up to a day and half each year in the lift going up and down. The rest of the time was spent going round in circles.

The whole building is a metaphor for the European Union: it is far too complicated, much too expensive, and has evolved without attending to the needs of its members.

When we arrived on the first day the good news was that there were a series of help-desks which were quite efficient. The key to each office was already in an envelope with each MEP's name on, and we only had to sign for it with no need to wait. There was another desk which gave out a personalised electronic voting card, and that was also quickly done.

This card was a key piece of equipment. Unlike Westminster, where MPs have to troop in and out of Ayes and Noes lobbies to be personally counted, most of the votes in the Parliament are by a simple show of hands. But when a precise count is needed, or when a 'roll-call' vote is called by any party, your card is essential. Without it you can't vote.

Inserted into a slot in front of your personal desk in the hemicycle – or indeed any other desk – this card identifies the individual and allows the vote to be recorded against your name. Fingers inserted into the gap below can press the left button for yes, the right for no, and the middle for abstention. The whole vote is over in seconds.

The key vote in this parliamentary session was going to be the vote for President of the Parliament, who would act like the Speaker of the House of Commons in presiding over the key parliamentary sessions.

This office is for two and a half years, with a new President appointed for the second half of the five-year Parliament. In the past, the two largest parties, the EPP and the PES, had agreed to take it in turns. The Socialists as the largest party historically always got the first term, with the EPP getting the second. The two block votes combined ensured that all the other parties were simply frozen out.

This time it was going to be different. The newly enlarged EPP/ED had decided to team up with the Liberals (the ELDR) and divide the two halves between them. This time it was the Socialists who would be frozen out of the Presidency complaining about a stitch-up – though they had been part of the earlier stitch-ups without complaining at all. The changes were starting early.

The rest of the week was taken up with detailed discussions determining who would chair which committee. Meanwhile my personal choices for committee memberships had been accepted. As a substitute member I would join the Environment Committee, where Green Tape was nearly as bad as Red Tape. But my main Committee, the undisputed source of the most Red Tape, was Employment and Social Affairs.

On my very first meeting I was in for a great surprise. I was expecting to see just the 40 or so MEPs who were on the committee, but there seemed to be about double that number of people. All round the sides, and in several rows at the back, were non-MEPs with cards in front of them saying who they represented.

I counted an extra 30 bodies, essentially for the Commission and the various political Groups. I approached an official and asked if it was correct that there really were 30 extras sitting in at every meeting. He replied: "No, there were usually more than that." Could one ever do business at all in such an environment, I wondered? I would soon find out.

The initial committee meetings were concerned with agreeing the procedures for grilling the candidate Commissioners when we returned from the summer recess. An early task was to decide the list of written questions from the committee for 'our' Commissioner-designate for Employment and Social Affairs, Anna Diamantopoulou from Greece.

Conscious of why I was there I proposed the question: "What priority would you give to promoting simplification and deregulation to lighten the burdens on business?" The Chairman put it to the vote, and it was voted down. This was obviously too radical a question. The committee was going to be a challenge, but the battle-lines had been drawn.

Meanwhile it was time to go home. I had been at work for a full three weeks, and it was time for the Parliament to shut down for the summer. I now had three weeks off.

On the flight home I asked the stewardess whether with my meal she could give me a miniature whisky unopened, as I would be driving. A hurried conversation with the purser ensued. I was then sternly advised that they could only do this if I declared the miniature at Customs on landing. Duty Free within the EU had finished, and this was the new ruling. I challenged this, saying that as British Airways had offered it to me free why should I have to pay any duty at all? They said it was not for them to reason why, they were just enforcing the new UK rules. It was not to be the last time that I would come across excessive and unique over-regulation by the UK.

Before we landed, the Captain announced the local time was "one hour earlier than Europe". I had thought that the UK was in Europe. Musing on this, I walked through customs without going through the red channel. I must confess now that I smuggled one whisky miniature into the UK. I had only been representing my country as a politician for three weeks yet already I had broken national law.

It was not long before I would commit a much more serious offence, and become an international criminal. But that was still in the future.

Chapter Four

Living with Lobbyists

In my previous jobs I regularly went on training courses and seminars on a variety of business issues. Most of these were suggested by my Chairman. He obviously realised how much I still had to learn.

As I was directly responsible for the progress of a business, and for the welfare of employees as well as of shareholders, regular training was certainly vital to keep up-to-date and to keep skills sharp.

I had naturally expected there would be similarly thorough training for those of us in the European Parliament, especially the first-timers. MEPs have the power to challenge proposed legislation, and to help re-shape it. We need to know what shortcomings to look for and how to find them. We need to know how to access expert advice to guide us, especially on key points of detail. We need to know how to craft amendments correctly in order to ensure that weaknesses in legislative proposals are precisely addressed. As a total political novice I was really looking forward to the various training sessions.

There weren't any.

My ultimate employer is the UK Government, but it makes no suggestions for training whatever. The political parties offer one form of training, namely how to handle the media: clearly dealing with spin is more crucial than dealing with substance. Otherwise there is nothing.

One can only assume that it must be generally accepted that immediately upon election politicians know all that there is to know. Or perhaps that we are completely untrainable.

In one single year the Environment Committee alone had handled 64 Directives. Some of them would have had over a hundred amendments tabled. One in particular I still recall, referring to the level of restrictions that should be placed on the use of octa- and deca-brominated diphenyl ethers. Of course we took the right decision, whatever it was: in any event it was determined by enthusiastic amateurs like me, with no experience whatever yet with the power to make laws Europe-wide.

Doesn't that worry you?

It should.

It sure worries me.

Into this training breach has stepped an army of lobbyists. At last count there were ten thousand in Brussels alone, the largest such army outside Washington DC. Their role is to hold each of us by the hand and guide us to the promised land of better laws – that is to say laws that better reflect their clients' particular concerns. Genuinely they can be very useful, though some rather less so than others.

Within weeks of taking office, I was invited out to dinner in Strasbourg by a particular lobby company. Their client was well represented: no less than five Divisional Directors had turned up, each one of whom was determined to give a separate presentation complete with slides. One half of the restaurant was laid out in theatre-style so that MEPs could face the screen and be bombarded with data. The other half was set out with tables laid ready for a sumptuous dinner afterwards – in this case a very long time afterwards.

I had mentioned to my hosts on my arrival that I might have to leave before the end of the meal. I was due to speak in a parliamentary debate at around 10.15pm that same evening. They said they did not expect this to be a problem. For them it wasn't.

Together with another dozen or so MEPs, I arrived for the briefing and a welcome drink at 7.30pm. Then followed the five dreary presentations, taking fully two hours. We sat down at table at 9.30pm. Ten minutes and no food later, my taxi arrived and I left for the Parliament.

I had been overloaded with information and definitely underloaded with dinner. I had received several thick folders and one bread roll. At least the bread roll had come in useful.

It may be natural for client companies, paying good money to lobbyists to flush out some malleable MEPs, to fill up every available minute once they have those MEPs corralled. They may also think that they have bought us for the evening so our time is fully at their disposal. They may feel it is necessary to lubricate their lobbying by offering a splendid repast in a flash restaurant. None of this is sensible.

MEPs don't expect to be well fed, or even to be fed at all - though if invited for a meal we do expect to get one. But we do look to spend our time usefully, which means being given a clear idea of key concerns, and a clear set of priorities for action. Too much information is frankly confusing, and MEPs are very easily confused.

Happily the approach from this particular company is not the general rule. Certainly a good dinner can be a welcome break and helpful for both parties. But generally such evenings work best when there are a very few hosts, equally few MEPs and even fewer pieces of paper. Such events provide the opportunity for bracing round-table discussions, thrashing out the pros and cons of contentious issues, and hopefully coming to a clearer mutual understanding of the really key points. A contact network is also then established so that either side can get in direct touch whenever the plot thickens – as it generally does.

The best lobbyists are those that come singly direct to your office in the brief windows of time between various meetings. You can then discuss issues on a one-to-one basis, and really get inside the subject. The very best go even further. They come early, when a proposed Directive is but a glint in a Commissioner's eye, well before the subject is due to come to the Parliament. They then reappear at intervals as necessary to comment on developments. Instead of just rehearsing the general arguments in favour of their own case, in due course they propose precisely how you should vote on specific amendments and why, and even give you the wording of amendments they would like to see tabled. MEPs don't have to agree with any of their arguments, or indeed accept any of their amendments, but it is highly helpful to have both. Life without such lobbyists would make our own work frankly much less effective.

Having said that, I have come across MEPs who have already served for one full five-year mandate and are convinced they know it all. I personally find their arrogance offensive, though I confess arrogance can easily come given so many people are always fawning over MEPs saying how grateful they are that such an important person can spare a few moments of precious time.

With any Directive, the devil is in the detail. Lobbyists can be of immense help, though you must be prepared to meet lobbyists representing both sides of the argument, and on occasion to sup with a very long spoon.

The lobbyists I like are prompt, professional and to the point. A 20-minute session gives plenty of time to do the business. Top of my list is the Engineering Employers' Federation.

The lobbyists I particularly dislike are the enthusiastic amateurs who think the best way to our hearts and minds is to jam our personal e-mail systems. Prior to a vote on the issue of Vitamin Supplements I received up to 100 e-mails a day instructing me how to vote. In the final few days this number rose to over a thousand just between midnight and breakfast: I counted them all in and I counted them all out. Many of them were from the same people, either Tom@elixir.health.com or his good friend Barb at the same address. Their mindless repetition of a demand for a nation-wide referendum on the key issue of freedom to buy however many vitamins they wanted progressively convinced me that they were nutters. They also increasingly convinced me that I was probably nuts myself to have been supporting their otherwise sensible cause.

I increasingly understand why normal people do not want to become politicians.

Having said that I do have some genuine sympathy with those who feel that their elected politicians are not listening to their electors - and that it is time they did. The secret is to find a way of making us listen.

I recommend to lobbyists that it is best to lobby friends rather than opponents, having first of course established who is which. Opponents will not usually be convinced by logical arguments, and their conversion may need a subtler approach. I have personally established one very good way to shake the certainty of UK Labour MEPs from their fixated support for yet more employment legislation. This is to orchestrate write-in campaigns by trade union members to complain about their likely loss of income – or indeed jobs – if a certain Directive were to be passed. The argument about job losses and extra costs when presented by the employers cuts no ice at all. When presented as individual letters by the workers themselves, especially when written to the many trade-union-sponsored Labour MEPs, the same argument suddenly has impact. Such campaigns are best organised by MEPs themselves lobbying their contacts back in the constituency.

This shows that MEPs are not just on the receiving end of lobbyists. We are all lobbyists nowadays.

Chapter Five

Coping with Constituents

I expected to have a very busy life as an MEP. But I did not expect to have at least two full-time jobs.

The Monday to Friday job is representing constituents in the European Parliament in Brussels or Strasbourg. Some people ask whether MEPs find the constant travelling is tiring. It's a fair question, though people are surprised by the answer.

I sometimes get up at around 4.45am on a Monday morning to drive to Birmingham airport and catch the 6.45 to Brussels. This means I can get to the Parliament by around 9.30 Central European time, (8.30 in the UK) when many people back home have yet to reach their workplace. If it is 'Strasbourg week' I arrive at my office there at around noon, via Frankfurt and a two-hour drive, though I still have to get up at around 5 am. That's another reason for not liking Strasbourg.

This routine is wearisome, but it is not exhausting. Generally I am back in the U.K. by Friday morning, or sometimes Thursday night. That's when MEPs start the second job, getting around the constituency. And that is where the travelling is indeed exhausting.

Thanks to Tony Blair's new P.R. system the eight West Midlands MEPs share one vast region. With 5.3 million people, it is larger than Scotland and indeed larger than several EU Member States. 59 Westminster MPs cover the same territory, but they each have their own separate patch. In the conurbations, that patch can be only a few miles wide and take a matter of minutes to cross. For MEPs to cross the West Midlands region to get to north Shropshire or south Herefordshire can take us two hours

– each way. There are usually constituency visits to make on Friday, Saturday and Sunday – not counting all the paperwork back home that has to be fitted in.

This second job can also be full-time.

MEPs from some other countries look at the Brits in amazement. Their weekends are free. Constituents, they say? Who are they? Such MEPs don't have the same schedule of visits, or the same volume of mail.

As Conservatives we are at least more fortunate than MEPs from other parties in the West Midlands region because there are four of us working as a team. We have roughly split the area into four quarters. Malcolm Harbour worked out a clever scheme whereby each of the four had a fairly equal balance of Tory seats & marginals, and town & country. This meant that I kept Shropshire and Warwickshire, but added the whole of Coventry. It still means I have twice the area of previous MEPs, who used to have their own separate eighth of the region.

Generally I handle constituency queries from 'my' quarter, and am the prime point of contact for organisations there. But the rest of the West Midlands expect to see each of its Conservative MEPs from time to time, just as Shropshire/Warwickshire/Coventry want to see the other three as well. So although this geographical split makes life a little easier, we are all still expected to traverse the whole region. I sometimes drive hundreds of miles at weekends. You need stamina for this job.

Under the previous electoral system, voters at least knew who 'their' MEP was. Despite that, many people used to complain that they never saw their MEP at all. Certainly MEPs had a difficult enough time being visible when they had a mere 800,000 people to represent. I imagine electors will complain even more loudly at the next election as we fail to be visible to all five million. We will have tried.

A further frustration for constituents – and for MEPs – is knowing who they should contact if they have a problem. In olden days they would write to their one MEP. Now they generally write to all eight. Within the

Conservative team we compare notes to ensure that we only send out one reply on behalf of the four of us. But the writer still expects a second reply from Labour and a third from the Liberal Democrats as well. So on balance each MEP is replying to a minimum of three letters where our predecessors only had to reply to one. Given that each letter may pose a problem that needs researching, and each takes time, the workload is trebled. Given there are not three times the hours in the day there has to be a danger that constituents will be served less thoroughly than in the past.

Replying to constituency queries is itself an art, and at an early stage I picked up a few helpful hints. A former member (of course not a UK Conservative) said that before replying to any constituent he would always check with his agent to see if the writers were paid-up party members. If they were, then the MEP would write a long reply in his own handwriting. If they were not, he would throw the letter in the bin.

Those who were binned were not best pleased, but they didn't matter. The members thought he was marvellous – and in this safe seat they held the key to his reselection…

Two other humorous hints concerned the phrasing of replies. Constituents always want to be assured that their worries were receiving prompt attention, even if they weren't. So one recommended response was 'I shall be sure to give the matter the attention it deserves'. A second suggestion was 'I shall waste no time in putting it at the top of my agenda'. Both can be read to imply extreme urgency: if anything they actually promise the opposite.

Certainly my own post-bag is rich and varied. The most regular contributors are the various councils, District, Borough, City and County, who obviously have shares in paper companies and have prompted our post-lady to have a bigger bike. I am frequently sent very thick, very glossy brochures, and literally inches of documents most earnestly compiled. I do try hard to read them, or at least scan them. But so many of the different councils have similar strategies for similar issues, covering jobs, tourism, attracting inward investment, transport, education, environment, health, housing etc., and send remarkably similar documents – of course produced independently by different people. There is huge multiplication of effort, all in the name of local democracy. No wonder councils are often themselves the largest local employer, often employing more people in a single council than the whole of the Brussels Commission.

One particular council, whenever it sends me yet more paper, kindly suggests that I file it in an appropriate place. I do, in a particularly appropriate place.

I also find it frustrating when the only European issue most Councils consider is how to apply for EU funding. So many of their policies and concerns have a European angle, even if they don't realise it. The recycling of old fridges – where the Government completely lost the plot, left Councils to pick up the bill and then blamed the EU – is but one of many such issues.

Apart from councils, letters come in surges on particular issues. Ritual and cruel slaughter of sheep in France. Human rights violations in Indonesia. Religious persecution in Egypt. Bans on Genetically Modified Foods. Problems of live animal transport. Bans on all animal testing for cosmetics. Restrictions on freedom of choice to buy vitamin supplements or traditional herbal medicines. Animal cruelty at Belgian livestock markets. Loss of investments at Lloyds. When bandwagons start to roll, the letters roll rapidly afterwards.

There's also a seasonal crop of letters and e-mails from students, which I tend to regard as rather cheeky. They probably find my replies even more so. Basically they write in to say that they have to submit a long thesis on some European matter, that they haven't started it yet, and please could I give 500-word answers to a series of questions. And by the way could I do this by return, as the whole thesis has to be submitted within the next ten days as the grand finale to their three years of presumed work. I give such students full marks for enterprise, and maybe send them some pointers, but no 500 words. Politicians may be elected to serve, but there are limits.

Then of course there are the pressure groups, the activists who send detailed questionnaires on very specific issues, demanding that I sign up to their manifesto without delay, and promising that my answers will be published widely for all to see. I do my best with these but, given that some of the questions are disarmingly over-simplified, a simple yes/no is usually impossible. My fall-back response is that I may be supportive of their general aims, but I only sign up to one manifesto: that of my party. It is on that and that alone that I was elected. I think that is a fair answer.

In amongst the pile are letters which raise meaty issues which I relish dealing with because I can help, and I can learn. These may be problems of property purchases in Europe which have gone wrong, cross-border pension issues, or simply visits to the Parliament. They may be companies asking for advice about how to do business in certain countries/markets within the EU. There may be queries about how different countries implement EU laws, or not as the case may be. They may be from people, or companies, concerned about aspects of new or current Directives.

I could cite so many examples of where well-meaning Directives have nearly gone off the rails, and threatened local businesses. Some of these will surface in other chapters but one example here will suffice: the Fresh Meat Directive. This was drawn up in response to the BSE crisis, and was designed to secure food safety and boost consumer confidence by ensuring product traceability from farm to fork. In other words, beef was to be labelled with country of origin, defining where the animal was born, bred and slaughtered. But as so often the legislation got carried away, with a key proposal suggesting that labelling on every piece of meat should also include the category of animal it came from, i.e. steer, heifer or young bull. This was the bright idea of France, which had such labelling domestically, though no West Midlands constituent had ever pleaded with me to establish the sex of their steak. Nonetheless our own Government as usual tamely went along with the French suggestion.

A large meat processing company contacted me in great agitation: such bureaucracy would increase costs by £50 per beast, and increase red tape without doing anything for food safety or the consumer. What could I do? Happily, in this instance I was already doing it, having tabled amendments to the key legislation and being programmed to speak in the forthcoming debate in the Parliament. I visited their north Shropshire site to go through the issues in detail, and was able to get good ammunition to support my amendments. I was able subsequently to put their minds at rest when the French proposal was quashed.

As a sideline I should record that my visit was personally frustrating in one respect. After a lengthy discussion, plus a full tour around the plant, I was invited to taste their primary product, and was taken into a room with platters of sizzling steaks. This was my idea of paradise. But after two token mouthfuls and before I could blink the steaks were all thrown away and I was ushered back to the boardroom for lunch. The lunch consisted of egg and tomato sandwiches. Paradise was lost very quickly.

Often the best way to deal with constituents' problems is to telephone them. It not only shows the personal touch, but it is quicker. At times it is a useful ploy in revenge.

On one memorable occasion a constituent's call late one night woke Angela up. The caller had just been watching the late news. He was disturbed at all the rioting in the Middle East and needed to talk to me urgently to see what I was doing about it. Angela rang me in my office in Brussels at 8 o'clock the following morning (7am UK time) to pass on the message. Half an hour later I had great pleasure in ringing this guy up, reminding him that he wanted to speak to me urgently and how could I help? After a pause, a drowsy voice replied that he had solved the problem. Arafat and Sharon might disagree that the Middle East problem was now fully resolved but I didn't argue. He has never phoned the house late again.

Finally there are those who contact their MEPs as a last resort. I have been surprised at the number of people who ring up asking how they can take some case or other to the European Court of Human Rights, because they feel that other roads to justice at home are blocked. If people have a local problem, be it heavy traffic passing by, lack of proper council house accommodation, or perceived environmental pollution issues, they go first to their local councillor. If they get no joy there, they go to their MP. If the MP says that there is nothing he/she can do they then write to their MEP(s) as if somehow we are more senior and have more clout regardless of the issue. When the MEP says there's nothing he/she can do either, because it is entirely a local matter, the writer becomes even more convinced that MEPs are quite useless.

I have been asked to check out EU availability of cheap sources of Viagra. I have also been pursued by old school friends ringing up out of the blue asking if they could have any of my spare tickets for Chelsea Flower Show or other such prestige events. As an MEP I apparently am thought of as being showered with such freebie invitations. It doesn't happen.

I have lost count of the number of telephone calls I have fielded from constituents wanting to 'go to Europe' on some local issue where the issue has not been resolved locally, or rather not resolved to their satisfaction. I am quite happy to tell people how to do this, but I do advise them against it. The European Court is not some catch-all court for every local grievance throughout the 800 million population of Europe: it doesn't have the resource and it doesn't have the role. Even if the European Court did consider every such grievance, a response would be years away.

In the vast majority of cases, if the issue is local the issue needs addressing locally. The problem is that the very existence of the European Court, or more specifically the recent Human Rights legislation, has encouraged every Tom, Dick and Harriet to try and go to the European Court every time they have any problem.

In any event, the European Court of Human Rights – odd though this may seem – is not even an EU institution. It covers the whole continent of Europe, not just the EU. The UK has signed up to its jurisdiction under a separate and earlier Treaty from our EU accession. Having said that, try and explain to constituents that this European Court is nothing to do with MEPs, and they will be even more convinced that MEPs are a waste of space.

That is one reason why MEPs don't often hold 'surgeries' in the way that Westminster MPs do. It is not that we don't want to meet the people: it is that the issues raised would so often be nothing at all to do with our role in the European Parliament.

The other reason is that often nobody would come. I remember an early outing to a major agricultural show, my attendance having been announced in the press in advance. On the day itself, an official said on the loudspeaker that the local MEP would be in the main office between 11am and 1pm if anyone wanted a word. I didn't expect a stampede, but I did expect a small queue. Farmers fed up with the Common Agricultural Policy, small businessmen fed up with increasing regulation, butchers, abattoir-owners etc., would surely all be falling over themselves to sound off about their problems.

During those two hours I had three cups of coffee and no visitors.

So I don't do surgeries, and use the time saved to go out and meet a lot more people.

Agricultural shows are actually just such an opportunity. I go to as many of these as I can, but no longer lurk in an office when I get there. There are literally thousands of people, and maybe scores of stall-holders, together with farmers and countryside organisations. They present great opportunities to catch up on the current issues, and to make and re-make key contacts. Sometimes there are unforeseen pitfalls. On one occasion I was judging the scarecrow competition (MEPs get all the really important jobs). Given I hadn't had time to get my hair cut, it was suggested I award myself first prize. Happily the press were out of earshot.

Apart from responding to letters I also initiate them – to local papers on local issues that wind me up. There's no shortage of issues, or of papers to write to. When I come home at weekends there's a pile of local/regional dailies ready to greet me:

The *Birmingham Post*
The *Coventry Evening Telegraph*
The *Shropshire Star*
The *Wolverhampton Express & Star*
The *Worcester Evening News*
....as well as a pile of weeklies:
The *Rugby Observer*
The *Leamington Observer*
The *Leamington Courier*
The *Redditch Standard*
The *Bromsgrove Standard*
The *Worcester Standard*
The *Kidderminster Shuttle*
The *Stratford Standard*
The *Stratford Herald*
The *Ludlow Advertiser*
The *Shrewsbury Chronicle*
The *Telford Journal*
The *Hereford Times*
plus various trade and business magazines.

Fellow MEPs may well have their own similar lists.

Although these are scanned for me as they come in, I still read through all of them personally on my return. There may be some angle or some issue that catches my eye, which needs to be followed up. Or there may be a letter to the editor from someone that prompts a reply.

So there's a fair bit to do at weekends, just dealing with letters and reading the papers. But all this takes second place behind going out into the real world of the constituency.

This I enjoy most of all. I particularly enjoy the social events with Conservative Associations: over the past year from a standing start I have made good friends with some lovely people. They also put on some splendid and happy events, ranging from drinks parties to very formal dinners. One of the side benefits is that my wife often joins me, which means we do see something of each other at weekends. It is a welcome change for her to leave not only the mail mountain but also the household chores, though she admits she often finds the rapid transition from Mrs Mop to Mrs MEP a trifle rushed.

On one particular Sunday we were together at a demonstration at Throckmorton airfield in Worcestershire, protesting against a proposal to build a new Asylum Centre in the middle of this rural community. Afterwards we were due to rush off to a posh lunch. While I drove local MP Peter Luff from one event to the other, Angela was quietly taking off her clothes on the back seat to change out of her sweater and jeans into a smarter outfit. Fortunately the policemen manning the various road junctions waved us through without a glance. Had we been stopped, all – literally – would have been revealed: two politicians in the front with a semi-naked lady in the back. The tabloids would have had great fun with that.

Wherever I am going I always try to get a detailed map in advance, even if I have been to the place several times before. Because of the large distances I travel I simply don't have the time to get lost. I even try and get maps of events, such as the various agricultural Shows, so that I can get to the right tent at the right time. This doesn't always work. On one occasion I was due at the Shropshire and WestMid Show in Shrewsbury, and was particularly pushed for time. I was due to meet our 'battlebus' which was parked in a particular row. Except it wasn't there. As we had been careful to ensure that it was equipped with a mobile phone to make contact easier, I brightly decided to dial the number. Phil Bradbourn answered immediately. Thankful to have located him I asked him straightaway: "Where exactly are you?" to which he replied "Nottingham". He had removed the 'phone for security reasons, as he didn't want to leave it in the bus overnight. Sometimes we were clearly better at teamwork than others.

Irritatingly, sometimes these various events can clash with suddenly arranged parliamentary business. A group of us were invited at short notice to fly out to Turkey as guests of the Turkish Government, just

With Wednesbury MP Betty Boothroyd at the opening of an extension of the Red Mill factory

From pork scrtachings to politics. The election result is announced at the National Indoor Arena, Birmingham. (From left: John Corrie MEP, myself, Malcolm Harbour MEP, Philip Bradbourn MEP)

On the campaign trail at an appropriately named pub in Shropshire
(above), and (below) in Worcester where we first realised we would win.

Canvassing in Stratford with Joyce Chadwick

With Birmingham constituents, discussing justice for Kashmir

The Member of the European Parliament
sash of office

*Welcome from Edward McMillan Scott MEP at the entrance
to the European Parliament in Brussels*

Speaking in the Employment Committee.
Bartho Pronk and Stephen Hughes (on the extreme left) look underwhelmed.

With Malcolm Harbour MEP (left) and Digby Jones of the CBI

Highlighting the Government's failure to deal with
EU Environmental Directives

Drawing attention to Socialist proposals on the Physical Agents
(Vibration) Directive which would mean farmers could only
drive tractors for two hours.

Drawing attention to the 'Rickety Ladders' Directive with Roger Helmer MEP

after a horrendous earthquake. The plan was for us to see the problems at first hand, and appreciate the extent of the international relief effort as well as the scale of the aid still required. This would give an on-the-spot perspective in a way that would never be possible without such a visit. We would also pay a lightning visit to the north of Cyprus, to see the problems of this beautiful but divided island from the point of view of the Turkish Cypriot community.

But I was already committed to speak at a Constituency dinner that same weekend. The tickets had already been printed and sold. I went to the dinner and passed up the trip to Turkey without hesitation. An MEP's prime loyalty is to constituents. Constituency Associations can cancel events at short notice, leaving a gaping hole in the diary: that is permitted. But MEPs cannot cancel their own attendance: that is grossly impolite.

Sadly not every constituent in the region is a Conservative. Well, not yet anyway. So it is important to reach out widely within the constituency beyond immediate supporters. This is never a problem.

Invitations pour in from businesses, from Chambers of Commerce, from local Councils, and from key groups such as the NFU. All need attention, and the challenge is always to programme them into the diary so that they make sense geographically on the same day if at all possible: you want to spend as much as possible at events meeting people rather than on the roads meeting traffic. It is also important to make sure that over time each Westminster constituency in the region gets reasonable coverage.

Invitations also come in for civic services in church, either for Remembrance Day, Judges' services, and multi-faith events or to celebrate the appointment of new local mayors. Tradition has it that every new mayor has a launch service in the local church, with all the 'touching' mayors as well - those mayors whose boundaries touch the territory of the mayor in question. So at these touching occasions there is a veritable mass of mayors. When these particular invitations arrive, the command is clear that 'chains will be worn'. Understandably, such civic guests are collectively known as the Chain Gang.

Now MEPs don't have chains, but I have discovered recently that we do have a sash of office. This is a very fetching piece of light blue silk, with the EU roundel in gold in the middle, and a gold tassel at the bottom. In common with EU legislation, it comes in a single one-size-fits-all version, regardless of your personal height or width. Apparently Brussels dress code dictates that it should be worn over the left shoulder diagonally to the right hip. I bought one, for the outrageous price of ₤60, and now wear it on such occasions trying not to look like the prat I feel. It confuses everybody, but is a good talking point at receptions afterwards.

As several of these services I have been amused by the common choice of a certain hymn by Charles Wesley. The fifth verse goes:

> Long my imprisoned spirit lay
> Fast bound in sin and nature's night:
> Thine eye diffused a quickening ray,
> I woke, the dungeon flamed with light;
> My chains fell off, my heart was free;
> I rose, went forth, and followed Thee.

I had visions of all these mayors with their chains falling off. I guess the local vicars shared the same sense of humour.

Apart from their chains, these dignitaries are generally also bedecked in robes. I was told proudly by one City Mayor that the new replacement robe this year (weighed down with gold braid) had cost £30,000. Another told me his chain of office was now worth £46,000. I recount this not as a criticism, simply as a fact. Such is part of our national and civic heritage. Yet if ever a Brussels Commissioner were to wear such an outfit there would be immediate condemnation of the extravagant waste of taxpayers' money. Mayors are local, so it seems to be okay.

Without a chain or a robe I must say I feel somewhat underdressed by comparison with the Chain Gang who stride as pairs of mayors down the aisle to sit in one of the many reserved rows. I also feel distinctly unloved when the prayers begin "For our politicians, whether local or in Westminster". No one prays for MEPs. We are either forgotten, or considered beyond redemption: I guess the latter. When the service is over I am also made to know my place as I thread my way on foot through the cavalcade of chauffeured cars, all ready to scoop up their respective mayor and on to the next event.

Having said that, I am very pleased to be invited. So often MEPs don't get asked to civic events because we are not front of mind, or maybe not on the right mailing list, or perhaps because the host is concerned that all eight MEPs might turn up. Anyway, the Westminster MP is regarded as the local representative apparently, not us. This reflects the MP's views too. I was once firmly but politely told by a long-standing Tory MP that it was custom and practice for him to be advised whenever an MEP was passing through his constituency. I replied that I would be delighted to oblige him if he in return would advise me whenever he was passing through mine.

Some of the invitations are self-generated, by which I mean that I simply invite myself. For example, it often never occurs to schools that MEPs might be interested to talk – and to listen – to their students. So I have to make the initial contact and take it from there. These can be very stimulating discussions, often including heated interventions by members of staff, so I try to do as many of these as I can. I particularly like to use these occasions to encourage students to think European for some stage of their further education. There are so many opportunities for study at European Universities, or even for positions as 'stagiares' in the Commission itself, and continental students already take much more advantage of this than we do. Such occasions are also useful for promoting the learning of other languages, not as foreign but as second or third languages.

In addition, I try to set up regular meetings with the local business community, as well as join in at existing meetings organised by Chambers of Commerce or Trade Associations. These often have problems specific to their industries but there is one universal refrain: can I please stop the mounting burden of red tape? When I explain to them that this is my mission, they are delighted. Because it enables me to contrast my mission with that of the Labour MEP red tape factories, I am delighted too.

There are other particular issues that I am interested in, such as the Environment. So again, I make the 'cold' contact to organisations such as English Nature, Friends of the Earth, Food Action groups and local nature reserves, and fit in a visit to them when I am in the area for other meetings. There will also be topical issues that need a rapid response. Sometimes these will be industrial, as a major business closes (or opens) or another crisis hits Longbridge. Sometimes they may be specific crusades, as amplified in the next chapter. Often the issues will be connected with agriculture, as more statistics hit the headlines about the problems faced by an industry increasingly ignored by the Labour Government. I have visited pig farms to draw attention to the plight of pig producers; I have campaigned for British beef outside local supermarkets; I also even found an opportunity to visit a pub on parliamentary business.

The *Evening Telegraph* had featured a pub near Coventry which was ditching its traditional 'Beaujolais Nouveau' day in favour of a 'British Beer and Beef-on-the bone' day. There was no way they wanted to support France given the continuing French ban on our Great British beef. I thought this was a wonderful idea, and rang them from Strasbourg to ask if I could pop in when the parliamentary session was over. The publican was delighted, and made me most welcome. What particularly pleased me was that the pub was not exactly in a traditional true-blue area, but everyone I spoke to still told the same story: our own UK Prime Minister had utterly failed to stand up for our UK interests in the beef war. They were very unimpressed with T. Blair Esq. I didn't need to persuade them who was responsible for letting France get away with it: they had already worked it out. I was glad I made the trip. The beer and beef were good too.

This story shows the benefit of keeping close to local news reports. I also make a special point of being in touch with editors and journalists themselves, and doing this personally rather than second hand via a press officer. This enables me not just to feed them stories but to get a feel of the stories they are running with, or about to run with, which might warrant a comment.

As an MEP it is quite a challenge to get any local press coverage. The whole raison d'être of local press/radio is local news. They can legitimately ask: what is the specific relevance of, say, the Chocolate Directive to the people of Shrewsbury? When the answer is that it is not absolutely specific to Salopians, but of great importance to everyone in the UK, back comes the answer: so it is not local news then, in which case we won't be printing it. In turn readers then say that they never read about MEPs in the local paper, which must mean we can't be doing any work.

The trick is to try and smuggle in European news disguised as local news, but this is easier said than done; alternatively to write regular columns in various papers, which I do – 14 of them. The softer option is to visit local events/shows/schools/farms/hospitals etc., in order to be seen in action in the locality, even if the activity is nothing much to do with Europe. Liberal Democrat MEP Liz Lynne is very good at this, for example campaigning for more than a 75p/week increase for pensioners. This has nothing at all to do with an MEP's responsibilities – but it does get a good press and shows that the MEP both cares and is in touch with real issues.

In my previous jobs I had always worked hard on media contacts, and developed strong links with all the grocery and catering trade press. As a result, the companies I worked for always had an above-fair-share of press coverage – and it was all free! I little thought how valuable this experience would be in the new strange world of politics.

By force of habit I monitor the press coverage closely to see if what I am doing is working. When it does work, it is a good way of giving feedback to constituents, and the large clutch of press cuttings each work confirms this is happening.

Initially this did not go down well with some of my MEP colleagues, who felt I was running a personal one-man publicity campaign. Given my lack of personal ambition for any grand political office nothing could have been further from my thoughts. There were many things I could not do in the political arena: this was one of the few talents I had, and I just wanted to spread the Conservative message as powerfully as I knew how. Happily this attitude changed when I was asked to help the entire team nationally with their own local press publicity in their own regions. This role I jumped at, and it seemed to work for them as well.

Further feedback comes when constituents actually come over and visit the European Parliament. Brussels is said to be the second most popular continental tourist attraction after Disney World: there are literally thousands of visitors pouring through every day on a carefully programmed basis. MEPs can subsidise the trip for up to 80 constituents a year. This is not a big number, but it helps. Visitors have a full tour of the building, have the chance to sit in on one or more committees, are thoroughly briefed on how the Parliament works, and then can grill one or more MEPs. These visits usually go down well, and do much to dispel some of the myths about what really goes on.

When such visits are over, I do encourage constituents to keep in contact, and to write to me on any issues that worry them. If they do write, I suggest they let me know if they are Conservative party members. It always helps to know. In return I always promise to give the issues they raise the attention they deserve. In fact I usually go much further than this and make a solemn commitment: I promise to waste no time whatsoever in putting their concerns at the very top of my agenda.

It is, literally, the least I can do.

Chapter Six

The Crusades

Whether or not MEPs deserve it, I soon discovered that we are taken pretty seriously by those in authority back home.

This means we can take up arms in what we consider to be good causes and actually get somewhere. Previous inexperience as a politician matters not a jot, though in-built impatience with bureaucracy can be a useful asset.

Sometimes MEPs may be able to advance these causes considerably even if they are not much to do with Europe. Sometimes we can simply help to keep the flame of hope alive. Most UK MEPs from each political party are active and vigorous crusaders: some of my own crusades are fairly typical, in that they grew out of local constituency issues where extra champions were sorely needed.

The First Crusade: Justice for Kashmir

This particular crusade started even before I was an MEP. When campaigning prior to the European elections in early summer 1999, I was introduced to a Mr Mohammed Suleman of Sparkhill in Birmingham.

He had started life in what is now Indian-occupied Kashmir. He had come to the UK as a youngster, but his homeland and his countrymen were always in his thoughts. He introduced me to a number of his close colleagues, all of whom were single-minded in trumpeting the cause of Justice for Kashmir.

Mr Suleman was to become one of my most constant correspondents, often calling Angela at about 7.30am on Monday morning when I was about to land in Brussels. Usually he wanted to talk me through the latest alleged atrocities, and invite me to yet another meeting with his colleagues. I had several such meetings as they had much pain to share with me. But I wanted to be more than just a sympathetic ear. I wanted to do something. There was not much I could do, but I could try.

This would have to be done with care. UK Foreign Secretary Robin Cook had already intervened with the Indian and Pakistani Governments with characteristic insensitivity, and proceeded to antagonise all parties with equal intensity. This was quite an achievement even for Robin Cook but not an example I wished to follow – though Jack Straw and Peter Hain would later show they were clearly happy to do so with their cack-handed treatment of Gibraltar in negotiations with Spain.

It was not only good politics to espouse a cause shared by so many West Midlands voters. It was also a hugely worthy cause in its own right. I was so aware that they had been battling ceaselessly and tirelessly for the liberation of their native country since 1947. Despite their efforts, precious little had changed in the following 50 plus years. I was very keen to help make a noise.

When I started in the Parliament I immediately joined the All-Party Group on Kashmir. This had regular meetings with other interested MEPs, and met with delegations of dignitaries from Azad Jammu Kashmir when they were visiting Brussels. It was also responsible for proposing Resolutions calling for India, Pakistan and Kashmir to sit down and resolve the issue. Given that both India and Pakistan had recently tested nuclear weapons, this continuing conflict could quite literally blow up at any time. The mutual military build-up in 2002 was yet to come, but would be no surprise.

My first opportunity for involvement came after Parliament had produced a firm but balanced Resolution condemning the violence and calling for action. This was circulating as a draft at the time of a lobbying day in the European Parliament by the Kashmir Freedom Movement, with Kashmiris from all over the UK descending on Brussels. I received an angry letter from the India Overseas Congress (I) UK saying that the Resolution was one-sided and biased, and failed to take the real facts into account. Apparently for it to be unbiased it should have concentrated on bashing Pakistan for alleged terrorist attacks. I didn't buy that at all. The country consistently failing to observe UN Resolutions was India. But to bash either side would simply aggravate the problem rather than produce a solution. I thought the Resolution was just fine.

The Friday after having received the letter, I took the initiative to telephone the Indian Ambassador to the EU. I wanted to get his reaction to the Resolution, to see if he agreed with the letter. To my surprise he offered to see me the following Monday in Strasbourg for a one-to-one meeting. That is one of the real benefits of being an MEP: you can access the key players very quickly.

His Excellency agreed with me that the Resolution was pretty fair. He would have tilted it perhaps 5% towards India, but he had no real complaint. He was keen to convince me that India wanted very much to see the dispute resolved. The very fact that he had been prepared to see me so instantly showed that India was very sensitive to outside opinion. This gave me great hope, and also lifted the spirits of my new friend Mohammed Suleman.

In due course my friend had an even better idea. He wanted to lead a Delegation to Brussels to meet personally with EU Commissioner Chris Patten. I advised him gently that this might be difficult as Chris was always jetting around the world, was seldom stationary for long, and had masses of people wanting to lobby him – which is probably why he was always somewhere else. But I agreed to try and set this up. Mr Suleman then rang me weekly (at times it felt like daily) to keep me on my toes. I hassled the Commission for a reply on a similarly regular basis.

My original request for a meeting had been in March 2001. Chris finally confirmed that he just would never be around long enough to meet us, but he would welcome a meeting in June with one of his Cabinet, Vicky Bowman, later to become Ambassador to Burma.

I passed on the good news and the visit indeed took place, with Mr Suleman's party of four driving over from the UK at dawn that morning to make their case at the one-hour audience. We were listened to with great attentiveness. Mr Suleman made the case for EU effort to kick-start the trialogue between India, Pakistan and occupied-Kashmir with great restraint and dignity. Copious notes were taken. The scale of the human rights issue was clearly recognised.

I was physically and emotionally embraced by the delegation after the meeting, with the group effusive in their thanks. By comparison with their ongoing efforts I had done but little. But if I had helped to plant the right seeds in the right place, I had given some help and some hope. I was thrilled to have done a bit of both. But the crusade must go on.

The Second Crusade: Matrix Churchill

The *Coventry Evening Telegraph* is a great crusading newspaper. Periodically it alights on some key local issue and give it the full glare of their publicity. As a regular subscriber to the paper, I kept on seeing regular comments about the ex-employees of Matrix Churchill.

Matrix Churchill's main claim to fame was its involvement in the Arms to Iraq affair. It was a highly skilled engineering company, ultimately Iraqi-owned, and a large percentage of its exports went to Iraq. Officially the products exported were innocuous, but suspicion steadily grew that the various products shipped could be used to bolster Iraqi weaponry.

The Managing Director had been trying to arrange a management buyout, but the day before his venture capital backers were due to sign the deal the UK Customs & Excise moved in and arrested him. The backers backed out. The buyout collapsed. Ultimately the company folded, throwing hundreds out of work with minimal compensation.

Some of the ex-employees committed suicide. Many never worked again. Their plight was not their fault, and the *Evening Telegraph* rightly called for justice.

74

Before the 1997 election, over 150 Labour MPs supported the campaign. They cried out that it was all the fault of the Conservative Government, and justice would be done if and when Labour were elected. After the election, 149 of the MPs went strangely quiet. Only local Coventry MP Jim Cunningham kept the faith and continued the campaign.

Certainly the Tories had something to answer for, and I felt an obligation to try and right a wrong. I also felt that there might possibly be an angle taking the case to the European Court of Human Rights because the ex-workers had tried and failed with the Government.

I phoned Conservative Central Office, to clear with them the fact that I was going to get involved. I said that the story was going to run on and on with or without my involvement, that it was perhaps better for the Party for me to get involved rather than stay in the wings. They accepted my argument, but their lack of enthusiasm was evident.

Before I could contact the newspaper, I was contacted by Christine Oddy – now ex-Labour as well as ex-MEP. She was going to sign up, and was I interested in doing the same? I said that she was a mind-reader. The following week we were both pictured co-signing the list of signatures, and the whole campaign got another lease of life.

The ex-workers had got themselves a small but vigorous committee. Chairman was Phil Harris, and Secretary was Tony Farrell. I was to have many meetings with them in the months that followed.

Tony showed me the outline of their case. It was very clear that the ex-workers were the innocent victims. What was less clear was who was guilty, and assuming it was the Government whether we could pin the blame firmly enough on them to get them to cough up.

The committee had been in touch with the Department of Trade and Industry, via Minister Kim Howells, without conspicuous success. His advice had been that if the committee could find firm evidence, his department would be very keen to look at it. But without access to all the official papers, there was no way that we could get such evidence.

Kim Howells was on a safe bet. This seemed immensely unfair.

With agreement of the committee I crafted a short list of very specific questions, and sent them off in my name for reply.

Meanwhile Labour MP Jim Cunningham had suggested to the committee it might be a good idea to work via a Labour MEP, Michael Cashman, instead. I had no objection to this, but said there was no point in dealing with two of us. Michael then apparently emerged from the woodwork, and with a nudge and a wink asked what the committee would settle for: would £1 million be enough? He allegedly said he was very close to the powers that be, and was confident that he could fix it. I do not know to this day whether Michael really believed this, or whether he was simply indulging in typical new Labour spin. But the result was that absolutely nothing happened, and having falsely raised the committee's hopes Michael disappeared back into oblivion. I was promptly invited back.

The main issue seemed to me as a non-lawyer that the Government had totally dropped the company in the mire. When the legal case against the company originally fell apart, as a result of the evidence of Minister Alan Clark, the interests of the employees were brutally ignored. When the Government was asked whether the Scott Inquiry into the affair would consider the interests of the workers, back came the answer that Lord Justice Scott had a wide enough remit to consider everything. But Scott himself, in his official Report, later said he had no remit to consider such an aspect. The ex-workers had been left on the scrap-heap and the Government, the Tory Government, had surely failed in a duty of care. This was a wrong I wanted very much to put right. The fact that the Labour Government had also failed to do anything, especially after all the promises in Opposition, made me doubly determined.

In the run-up to the General Election in 2001, I asked Shadow Home Secretary Ann Widdecombe for her support. She offered sympathy but said it was a matter for the DTI. I then had a meeting with Shadow Secretary for Trade and Industry David Heathcoat-Amory. All I could get him to commit to was to say that we would look at it again when we had won the Election. It was a start, but not too helpful when we lost it.

Meanwhile, the ex-Managing Director of Matrix Churchill, Paul Henderson, was considering filing a personal claim against the Government, and suggested we contacted his London lawyer to compare notes. This we agreed to do, and I flew back from Brussels for a meeting with him, Tony and Phil. The lawyer kindly said he would consider whether he could help put together a formal claim for us on a no-win/ no fee basis, and gave some helpful guidance on formatting the documentation we already had.

We were further encouraged when Paul Henderson's individual claim was accepted in principle: the sum awarded would not be determined before late 2003 at the earliest. We agreed to hang on for his result, and then hopefully piggyback on his success with our own claim. At the time of writing, we await the outcome of this next stage.

Tony and Phil then called a meeting of the ex-workers to seek their approval for this course of action, which was gladly given. The ex-workers had huge confidence in their committee. So have I.

The Third Crusade: Have a Heart

As the only West Midlands MEP from any political party on the Environment, Public Health and Consumer Policy Committee in the European Parliament, I take a close interest in health matters.

In early 2001 I visited the University Hospital NHS Trust in Birmingham to get myself updated on their priorities and progress. I was very impressed that Princess Anne would shortly be opening the first phase of the Centre for Defence Medicine in Birmingham: as well as being the UK Centre, it was seen as the model for all of NATO. Not for the first time, Birmingham was showing the way in Europe.

I was also reminded that the University Hospitals at Selly Oak and Edgbaston were recognised as amongst the premier teaching hospitals in Europe, and that Birmingham also hosted the largest organ transplant unit in the whole of the EU. What I was told next concerned me greatly.

On heart transplants specifically, there were currently seven centres in the UK. The powers-that-be had decreed that it would be better if there were only four in order to concentrate resources. The general belief was that three had already been identified: two in London/South East and one in Newcastle-on-Tyne. The fourth was officially a toss-up between Manchester, Sheffield and Birmingham, each of which did around 35 such transplants a year. New centres were expected to do about 80.

Sheffield had the weakest case for survival: Manchester was the longest established and rumoured to be the favourite. The other rumour was that the decision against Birmingham had already been taken, but was being cynically sat on until after the General Election to help Labour MP Gisela Stuart, then a Health Minister, to hold on to her marginal seat of Birmingham Edgbaston.

This was certainly worth a crusade.

My position was not just blind belief in Birmingham. The fact that Birmingham had the largest total transplant unit in Europe meant that Birmingham was a magnet for gifted surgeons. A whole infrastructure of medical expertise had grown up around this including advanced research programmes: this in turn helped the quality of the teaching hospitals. It would be a disaster if this were all put at risk as a result of a decision on heart transplants in isolation.

It was also absurd that Birmingham was part way through a multi-million pound investment in the Queen Elizabeth Hospital, including a state of the art cardiac unit. Apparently the Committee responsible had not be allowed to consider any of this in their deliberations. So much for joined-up Government!

It would also be outrageous, if true, that the decision had already been taken but suppressed for electoral reasons. With a General Election coming up, this was a big news story.

As I had a fortnightly feature column in the *Birmingham Post*, I decided to air the issue as powerfully as I could in my next article. The delay in the Government announcement did give us a chance. I suggested the *Post* mount a huge headline-grabbing campaign. If the West Midlands region spoke with one vigorous voice, we could yet secure victory. Certainly the securing of Birmingham's position as the pre-eminent total transplant centre was worth fighting for.

To be fair, the *Post* had trailed the outline story a couple of weeks earlier, though hadn't made much of it. I spoke to the editor, Dan Mason, and he became very excited about building this into a major campaign, and decided to give it everything he'd got this time around. Within a few months the campaign really started – though ironically one of the early features was a full page of all the Birmingham MPs who were supporting the campaign, without any mention of any MEP at all.

I chided Dan about this, and he graciously corrected the oversight the following week mentioning my own role. To his credit he then thought of another great idea, that I should try and get other MEPs from adjacent regions to climb on board in support. This was no problem. Jonathan Evans as Conservative MEP for Wales was delighted to sign up; Birmingham was much closer than Manchester for most of his constituents. Best of all, Dr Caroline Jackson from the South West Region was also supportive, particularly on behalf of her constituents in Gloucestershire. As Caroline was Chairman of the Environment and Public Health Committee, her signature carried extra weight. She was also more than happy to copy her letter of support to Health Secretary Alan Milburn.

Apart from the relentless headlines in the Post, the issue went quiet after the Election, and stayed quiet for several more months. One day on arriving back at Birmingham Airport I was greeted in the newspaper shop by the happy headline: 'QE transplant unit saved!'

This was wonderful news. Many people had a hand in the result. It is because so many did that we got the result we wanted and deserved. I do not believe to this day that it was the decision the Government had intended.

The Fourth Crusade: Birmingham as European Capital of Culture

Each year, one major city in the EU is chosen as European Capital of Culture. This is a highly prestigious award, and very good for business. The Commission has decided that in 2008 the title should go to a city in the UK. It would be up to the UK Government to determine which city.

The initiative to propose Birmingham was taken by Birmingham City Council, or rather the current ruling Labour clique, without reference to any other political group at all. Councillor David Roy, the Conservative Group Leader, was not impressed. He was also not surprised: cross-party consensus-building had never been high on the local Labour agenda. The Conservatives nonetheless agreed to support the bid, as did the Liberal Democrats.

All eight MEPs were invited to the launch of the bid - albeit at such short notice that most of us couldn't make the event. All wished to back the bid, though our advance support was not canvassed either. I wrote to Labour Group Leader Councillor Albert Bore asking for more details ahead of the date: typically I never had a reply.

A fortnight before the launch I also wrote to Labour MEP Simon Murphy, and to Liberal Democrat MEP Liz Lynne. My suggestion was that all West Midlands MEPs should lock together in support of the bid on a genuine cross-party basis as this should strengthen the bid's chances. Specifically the thought was that one MEP from each of the three parties should be the prime point of contact for keeping colleagues informed. Having grown up as a Brummie I was keen to see the bid succeed.

Liz replied promptly and positively. She was delighted to be the Liberal Democrat contact point. As an active Member of the Culture Committee in the European Parliament, and with a history of 22 years on the stage before entering politics she was well qualified for the role.

Two weeks later I had a reply from Simon agreeing to my suggestion, saying that Michael Cashman would be in touch. Michael too was well qualified given his high-profile TV career, though he never responded.

My column in the *Birmingham Post* made the point that the Birmingham bid had so much going for it. To win, we needed not just to have the best bid: we had to manage the politics in Westminster and Brussels better than anyone else. Brian Woods-Scawen, as Chairman of the Bid Group, was keen to have strong cross-party political support. I assured him personally that he now had it. The fact that Labour never sought it was now history: we needed to look to the future, and to work together for Birmingham's success.

The first meeting in Brussels with the three MEPs, Stephen Hetherington the bid co-ordinator and Brian Woods-Scawen, soon took place, and the show was now on the road. Sadly a few months afterwards the bid team presented its case direct to Downing Street, surrounded by Labour politicians, without any reference to other parties at all. The first time that Liz Lynne and I knew anything about it was when we read the news in the *Birmingham Post*.

We chose not to make a public issue of this at the time as we had no wish to weaken the bid further. But for the bid team to have denied the cross-party support which would have so strengthened the bid, in order for the local Labour group to get all the glory, was immensely short-sighted. We exchanged some curt words with Brian and Stephen, and later they both came out again to Brussels for a special visit to myself and Liz. They made it clear that the Downing Street launch had been planned to be just with a swarm of local children, but that at the last minute Labour MEP Michael Cashman decided to insert himself on his own initiative without reference to the bid team. We should not have been surprised.

The decision was in the gift of the Prime Minister, and announced in mid-2003. If the final choice had gone to the strongest bid, then Birmingham would have won - as indeed the other contenders expected. However the assessment panel was briefed in the end to award the prize to one of the weakest bids, to the city of Liverpool, simply because it had the greatest need of the financial rewards the title of Capital of Culture would generate. Ultimately the decision was entirely political. We should not have been surprised at that either.

The Fifth Crusade: Saving the Green Belt

Although I was brought up in a city, I have always felt drawn to the countryside. In recent years I had become most concerned how much the rural way of life across the region was under threat from the urban-dominated Labour Government, led by 'Tony the Townie'. I determined to use what clout I could conjure up to play an active part in safeguarding the rural way of life, and in protecting what remained of our countryside.

Initially I was happy to play very minor supporting roles, such as helping mid-Worcestershire MP Peter Luff save the community of Throckmorton from being submerged by a new Asylum Centre for would-be immigrants, and later joining the Countryside March for Liberty & Livelihood together with some twenty Conservative MEP colleagues. But I soon had the opportunity for a larger role almost on my own doorstep.

In summer 2002 the Government announced it was starting a lengthy consultation process on the future runway requirements of air transport during the coming thirty years. Included amongst the options was an idea to build a gargantuan new international airport, obliterating two lovely villages near Rugby. Capable of handling around 70 million passengers a year, it would be the second largest airport anywhere in the world. Such a plan would save building extra runways elsewhere, especially in the South-East, though it would also involve closing Birmingham International Airport completely.

I felt this proposal to be self-evidently absurd. Cynically I even suggested to one local newspaper that the idea had only been put forward so that the two MPs for Warwick and Rugby, both Labour marginals, could appear to be local champions if they opposed it and the idea was subsequently withdrawn. I then went on holiday.

When I returned a few weeks later, I found that local action groups had been started, money was being raised for a high-profile campaign, and there was a genuine fear that such a proposal might actually happen. The joke quote ascribed to John Prescott: 'The Green Belt is Labour's proudest achievement, and we intend to build on it', didn't seem so funny any more. With this Government it really seemed possible.

As a member of the Environment Committee in the European Parliament I waded in immediately to buttress the local campaign. I stated that such a proposal would be environmental vandalism on a massive scale. I secured the support of all the region's MEPs irrespective of political party. I wrote to the Environment Commissioner, reminding her of what she had said at the recent Johannesburg Earth Summit, that political leaders had to show not just the vision but also the will to safeguard our environment for future generations. I wrote to newspapers across the region, and contacted County, Borough and District Councils to get their backing.

The main hard work was being done by unsung heroes on the Anti-Rugby Airport Committee (ARAC), and by separate village Action Groups. But I seemed to be generating a lot of the publicity. and when I said I would join the protest March in October that year ARAC asked if I would be the only speaker at the end of the rally.

I was delighted to accept, and later to do a repeat performance in June 2003 to keep the campaign in the headlines. This was now increasingly necessary because the High Court had decreed that the Government had acted unlawfully in excluding Gatwick from the original consultation. This meant that the consultation period had to start all over again, and now be extended to end June 2003, with the verdict unlikely to emerge before early 2004. For fully 18 months, the villagers in the affected communities lived under a shadow. They did not deserve to have their rights trampled on in such a way, especially as a result of Government incompetence.

I was heartened that I could help champion so worthy a cause, and thrilled to work alongside a veritable army of champions in all the local villages and towns.

Meanwhile there is no doubt that the Government will rightly be pilloried for having failed to rule out such a grotesque proposal at a much earlier stage, especially as they had initially refused to accept their consultants' own preferred choice – the extra runway at Gatwick that was never even considered. We have no doubt that we shall prevail.

*

The above are illustrations of typical crusades. MEPs don't have to get involved in the extra work of such campaigns, but most of us generally do. It may sound quaint and old-fashioned, but most politicians do actually enter public service to serve the public.

Of course I don't expect readers to believe me. After all, why should anyone believe a politician?

Chapter Seven

What does an MEP stand for?

Some crusades can be more provocative than others.

Many politicians like to keep their head down and keep their noses out of trouble. That is no fun at all. I maintain that even fledgling politicians should stand up for what they believe in – always assuming they do believe in something. I did and I do.

In one specific case it probably cost me a number of votes locally. My offence? I dared to campaign in favour of genetically modified (GM) crop trials rather than take the populist line of condemning 'Frankenstein Foods' outright.

As a member of the Environment Committee I was anyway caught up in the debate. It was an environmental issue – would GM crops really cause unknown and permanent environmental damage?

Within my first year as MEP I had read widely and deeply on the subject, and had become progressively convinced of the potential of GM crops. Not only could they be good for the biotech companies, and also for farmers with improved yields: above all they could in theory be positively good for the environment because less herbicides and pesticides would need to be used. But I needed to be convinced of this literally on the ground.

So one summer I went walkabout in the West Midlands.

My first visit was to a public meeting in Warwick, as a special addendum to the Annual General Meeting of Warwickshire County Council. The public gallery was full. There were various names that I recognised from letters in the local press. There were a number of parish and district councillors from around the county.

There was also someone dressed as a bee.

The first speaker said that science could make mistakes. True. Friends of the Earth (FoE) said that GM crops were not seen as relevant to the consumer. Also true. A Green from Stratford said that organic farming was the way forward. Not true, as such practices could never feed the nation. But all such interventions were loudly applauded. The general mood was clear.

It was reflected in the summing up by a Labour Councillor: there was considerable mistrust and concern about the whole principle of GMOs; the so-called science was questionable because such research was all funded by multi-nationals for their own interests; given the uncertainty, we should exercise the 'precautionary principle', which meant if in doubt don't do it. Finally he wanted Warwickshire to be a GM free zone. The last comment got the loudest applause of all.

Meanwhile the exact opposite view was being claimed by the UN, listing the benefits of such staple crops as GM rice, millet, sorghum and cassava as follows: "These varieties have 50% higher yields, mature 30 to 50 days earlier, are substantially richer in protein, are far more disease and drought-tolerant, resist insect pests and can outcompete weeds. They will be especially useful because they can be grown without fertiliser or herbicides, which many poor farmers can't afford anyway."

The report concluded unequivocally that apart from environmental benefits, such GM crops could help to stave off malnutrition for upwards of 800 million people worldwide.

It sounded too good to be true. Was it? Who was right? Would the impact be the same in the UK? Well, that was the purpose of the trials. It was also the purpose of my seeing for myself what was actually happening in the trials literally on the ground.

Before I could get to my first field another negative story hit the press. Again Government incompetence made it worse. One small seed company, Advanta, found out that some GM seed had accidentally got mixed in with conventional rape seed. A 'contaminated' batch had got out and was already under cultivation. The moment Advanta found out they immediately went to the Government. The Government did nothing for a month before finally, and unilaterally, deciding that the affected crops should all be destroyed. Advanta only learnt about this decision when they read it in the newspapers.

They had apparently been trying for the whole of the four intervening weeks to organise a follow-up meeting with the Ministry. When I spoke to them later they were still trying, but the Civil Service was all on holiday to celebrate the Queen Mum's birthday, and the Secretary of State for Agriculture was terribly busy doing something or other in Portugal.

It was clear that the Government was not on top of the problem. The problem was on top of, and at the top of, the Government.

I then went to Worcestershire to look at GM sugar beet. These trials were monitoring insect, butterfly and beetle populations. I saw the profusion of insect traps throughout the crops that were regularly inspected and their contents counted. Like rape, normal sugar beet is often feebler than the weeds that grow around it. The safest and most effective general purpose weedkiller, widely available under many names but generally known as 'Roundup', cannot be generally used because it kills the beet as well. Roundup is so safe that if it is sprayed on water you can then safely drink the water. This is not however recommended.

GM Sugar beet has been modified to carry an extra gene from naturally occurring bacteria living in the soil. GM beet is resistant to Roundup which means it can be used after all – and the good news being that it needed less frequent applications that the alternative chemicals which should be better for the wildlife as well.

On my visit the beet was looking extremely healthy. The insects appeared to be having a good time too.

My next trip was to Shropshire. The local farmer very nearly hadn't gone ahead with the trials as Government dithering in the Spring meant that approval came eight weeks late. He had nearly missed the growing season altogether.

However, all was now proceeding according to plan. The National Institute of Agricultural Botany (NIAB) had been responsible for all aspects of the trials, including the drilling and the spraying. British Sugar would again be responsible for harvesting and disposing of the crop, and the control systems seemed to be operating flawlessly.

A few weeks later I was in the county again at another farm, where I was joined by a local beekeeper Richard Monbiot. Richard had apparently been hostile to start with because he was concerned that GM pollen might contaminate his honey. But now he was a staunch convert. He later gave me a statement which said, amongst other things:

"I find nothing to alarm me as an individual or as a beekeeper in relation to the GM crop trials under way. I cannot give a blanket approval for anything that might not yet be in the public domain. However I consider it to be highly advantageous in principle that GM development can facilitate the reduction of herbicide and insecticide use and that my bees would benefit from a lower frequency of application....

...Most of the hysterical opposition is whipped up on apocryphal and alarmist stories which do not bear examination on a rational basis. It is right that all development in this area should be closely monitored and evaluated to prevent abuse and dangerous application of the science. But there is no place for opposition for its own sake. I actually find it an interesting and exciting technology."

He said I was free to use his statement, and use it I certainly did.

The farmer gave me the best reason yet why organic farmers in the UK, and certification bodies such as the Soil Association, hated GM crops with such intensity: he suggested that their concern was not because the environment might be damaged, but precisely because it might not be damaged. Success for GM crops, with minimal chemical use, greater benefit to the environment and lower cost of production, would undermine the whole rationale for organic crops. This was so blindingly obvious I was ashamed I hadn't rumbled it before.

In August the National Agricultural Centre in Warwickshire was due to host a major briefing by the Royal Agricultural Society of England on the subject of GM crops. Although it was essentially a closed meeting for the agricultural world I managed to get myself invited.

The debate was led by a British scientist working at the heart of the US biotechnology industry as head of the US Plant Sciences Institute. He attempted to address the question of why biotech was generally embraced over there but distrusted over here.

He expanded on some of the misinformation abounding, one example of which concerned the Monarch Butterfly. A test had been done with butterfly larvae placed on milkweed dusted with GM pollen. The larvae all died. Therefore GM crops were presumed to be dangerous to beautiful butterflies.

This was most misleading research. It was true that Monarch butterflies were normally brought up on milkweed. But milkweed grows on roadside verges, not in the middle of crops, and anyway pollen appears at a completely different time of year to the butterfly breeding season.

This didn't stop Greenpeace filing a suit against the Environmental Protection Agency. The case was thrown out. Not only was no valid data found to show any adverse effects on butterflies: available scientific evidence actually proved the opposite, that such crops had a positive ecological effect when compared to likely alternatives. The collapse of the Greenpeace case didn't stop the original story resurfacing in the UK press time after time.

His speech was followed by Jonathan Curtoys from the Royal Society for the Protection of Birds. He said that the RSPB had no objection in principle to GMOs. He reminded us at the end of a fascinating talk that birds were declining anyway as a result of modern farming practices. He could have added that farmers were a declining species too.

His final almost throwaway remark astounded me. He said his only sources of regular information on GM issues were Greenpeace and FoE. Nothing regular from the industry, nor from Government. I wondered if his organisation was typical, and suspected so. The case against GM was having a clear run. If only someone would speak out on the other side.

Within a few weeks the spotlight fell on me. A new round of GM crop trials for autumn plantings was announced. One farm was within walking distance of my home, in downtown Harbury. I was suspected of being the direct cause of this environmental evil being inflicted upon the village. The argument went that I was known to support such trials, so my home village was obviously an acceptable place for them to happen. I was flattered people thought I had so much influence, but frustrated that another baseless rumour was gaining such wide circulation.

One of the locals was particularly uptight, and I had every sympathy for his predicament. John Home was the proud proprietor of Fosse Way Honey. His bees were based within a mile of the trial field. The Soil Association, the self-appointed guardians of organic purity, had decreed that for honey to be certified organic beehives had to be at least six miles away from any GM crops. This was a completely arbitrary rule that I suspected was simply to do with limiting the number of GM crop trial sites. But supermarkets accepted this rule, so John had to comply. The question was: who would pay to move his hives?

I took up his case with the seed companies. Not their problem apparently. I wrote to the Secretary of State asking for compensation. I finally managed to prise out a reply fully three months later saying that the six-mile limit had no basis in law (which I knew anyway, but which didn't address the problem) and that 'liability for any loss as a result of the actions of another is a matter for the courts.' I called John to confirm the bad news. As he was away, I wrote him a letter. Given I was not his favourite person I didn't expect a reply: I was not disappointed.

In the meantime much resentment had been whipped up locally – not against the Labour Government who had put the trials in place, not against the nearby Labour MP James Plaskitt who chose to remain remarkably inaudible on the issue, but against me because I had dared to support GM crop trials. It was all apparently my fault.

There was a packed Parish Council meeting in Harbury Village Hall calling for the tests to be called off. I was away in Brussels at the time but later a University student, who was writing up the issue as a project, came round to my house to quiz me. He also filled me in on what had happened. He had been amazed how emotions had run so high at the meeting, and how the facts about the potential benefits of GM technology seemed to be deliberately suppressed. He told me that he spoke to someone there who said he was from FoE: he allegedly admitted that it was not in their interest to bring out the facts as that would have undermined their campaign.

Before the village meeting there had been a demonstration in the road outside my house. There were around forty protesters, only five of whom came from the village. The rest came by car from places unknown. The organisation called itself RAGE, or Royal Action against GM Evaluation: I hadn't realised the Queen was a supporter. After the protest they went off to invade the GM farmer's field for an organic picnic, plastering all the lamp-posts and post-boxes en route with RAGE stickers. Given their effective stickiness the village remained defiled by these so-called defenders of the natural environment for many weeks afterwards.

But the protest made clear the answer to the question: what did MEP stand for? One protester, whose photograph was splashed over the local press the following day, had proudly held a placard stating: My MEP stands for More Environmental Pollution.

At least it was different from the usual message. People normally think that MEP stands for More Expenses Please.

Chapter Eight

Very Red Tape

The main work of an MEP within the Parliament itself is to consider proposed EU legislation, dissecting and amending as appropriate.

Some such legislation is indeed to be welcomed, wherever it helps to establish a level playing-field to complete the Single Market and promote jobs. The trouble is that not all such legislation is in this category. At the other extreme, Employment and Social Affairs legislation is in a class all of its own in putting extra burdens on business at the direct expense of job promotion.

Most sensible people steer clear of the Employment and Social Affairs Committee because this is where the Red Tape is mainly generated. It was exactly the reason I wanted to be there. To my delight, the day I joined I was asked by our Leader to be the Conservative Spokesman for this key area.

Given the lack of business people in politics, I suspected this Committee might not have the needs of business and the promotion of jobs as its highest priority. I was certainly right. But I'd assumed the problem would be Commission proposals for more and more red tape, with most MEPs rubber-stamping them out of ignorance of the business impact. Here I was certainly wrong.

The MEPs on this Committee are more interested in Social Affairs than Employment. With a few exceptions, the Committee has attracted lefties from all political parties. Their clear priorities are strengthening the rights of workers and the role of trade unions. Most of them believe that business is bad, that Big Business is very bad, and that Multinational

Big Business is the ultimate evil. Their contribution to Commission proposals for more Directives is therefore to welcome them and propose amendments to make them tighter still. They conclude that employees need to be protected from their nasty employers: given that most of these MEPs have never been employees (who would ever employ them, one wonders?) it is curious that their minds are made up with such certainty.

The above may sound an exaggeration. It really isn't. Neither is it an exaggeration to point out that UK Labour MEPs are the leftest of the lot.

At our regular monthly meetings, I sit on the front row facing the Chairman and the Secretariat. I try to convince visitors that this is recognition of my importance as Spokesman: they soon notice that I sit between Bastos and Cocilovo, and that alphabetical order might have something to do with the seating plan.

The two people dead centre of the front row defy the alphabet because they really are important. They are the Co-ordinators for the two largest political groups, responsible for co-ordinating and steering the votes across all group members. Bartho Pronk is 'my' Co-ordinator on behalf of the EPP/ED. The Co-ordinator who sets the direction for the whole Party of European Socialists is UK Labour MEP Stephen Hughes.

The son of a Durham miner, Stephen's old Labour blood runs proudly through every vein. Although he is actually a very pleasant guy, devoid of spin and easy to work with, I disagree absolutely with almost everything he says. In turn, he never minds disagreeing with Labour Government Policy back home. He also never minds admitting it.

I guess he therefore doesn't mind that I tell everyone else. Businesses need to know who they have to thank for all the extra red tape and social legislation coming out of Brussels. One of our own Labour MEPs should take full credit, and I believe in giving credit where it is due.

In September 2001, the UK Minister for Europe, Peter Hain, came out to Strasbourg to talk to any UK MEPs prepared to listen. He urged us not to undermine the Common Position of the European Council on the issue of Information and Consultation when it came before the Parliament. Member States had agreed a fragile text that all countries could just about live with. The UK didn't want to see this unpicked with nasty amendments from us.

I responded to say that he could indeed rely on the Tories. But could he rely on the Labour MEPs? He swatted my comment aside and said of course that could not be a problem.

Suspecting otherwise, I accosted Stephen after the meeting. He confirmed he would be seeking to toughen up the Common Position in three key areas. He wanted the imposition of sanctions for non-compliance, the proposals to be implemented sooner, and the tightening of voluntary procedures so they were effectively compulsory.

I immediately wrote to Peter Hain telling him the bad news. He never replied – but then as his visit had been simply an exercise in spin for the media back home I was not surprised.

The day before the important vote on the Directive, I hosted a special working lunch in Brussels for the Involvement and Participation Association. This organisation was fully dedicated to employee information and consultation. But the point was that all their member companies had different needs. Their trump card was that John Lloyd, the Trade Union representative from the AEEU, was one of the speakers. He was clear that a one-size-fits-all solution could never be the answer.

I had invited all the Committee to come and hear this at first hand. Three Labour MEPs said yes, but none of them arrived. Their minds were already made up. When the time came, Stephen led his Group in voting through Socialist amendments that the CBI immediately described as 'hugely damaging'. I ensured that the main votes were all roll-called, so that the votes of individual MEPs would be identified on the record.

One of his Stephen's early tasks was a Report on the proposed Extension of the Working Time Directive to Mobile Workers (that's lorry-drivers to the rest of us). Again the UK Government wanted us all to vote a particular way. Again Stephen was keen that the Government should have the benefit of his superior views.

He proposed amendments that would have cut down night-time driving hours, and also include self-employed drivers, a category that many Member States specifically wanted excluded. In every respect Stephen took a different line to the Government: he also took a different line to the industry. The UK Road Haulage Association said that Stephen's amendments 'showed no understanding of the needs of the industry nor its employees.'

Before the final vote in plenary I managed to orchestrate a campaign with distribution companies back in the UK: droves of their drivers, all union members, wrote personal letters to Stephen complaining how a cutback in night-time work would hurt their earnings. He later said to me he was surprised how many letters he had received. I agreed it was really most astonishing.

At the plenary session in Strasbourg I called a Press Conference, flanked by MEPs from Austria, Finland, Sweden, the Netherlands and Greece, condemning moves that would make our industries less competitive. It was reassuring to be able to show that we were giving a clear lead to others on this issue. It was also important to show that the UK Conservatives were not alone.

The problem is that Stephen is not alone either. One of his colleagues is Richard Howitt. A worthy champion of minority rights, he is also a great lover of legislation. He successfully fought to become the Parliamentary Spokesman or Rapporteur on the Commission Green Paper on Corporate Social Responsibility (CSR). This covered the obligation of Companies to be good employers and to embrace policies that were good for the environment, as well as to be profitable.

I fought successfully to become the EPP/ED shadow Rapporteur, to mark him every step of the way. He believed that all companies should operate CSR within a prescribed one-size-fits-all regulatory framework. I regarded this as complete cobblers, to use a technical Parliamentary term.

Over the following months Richard was tireless in arranging meetings with interested parties, including calling a special Conference with around 1,000 delegates. Speaker after speaker declared opposition to his ideas for legislation. At the end Richard summed up, thanking them for the high level of support for his ideas and their welcome of legislation.

I lost count of the businesses that asked me whether Richard was simply being a typical Labour politician and not listening, or was simply not understanding.

Fortunately on this issue the whole EPP/ED Group were on my side. So were the Liberal Democrats. This gave me the confidence that we could do much to blunt his proposals. I tabled a mass of amendments, many of which passed.

On the key vote that voluntary should prevail over compulsory I decided to play hardball. I said that if this did not prevail, the whole of the EPP/ ED and ELDR would vote against the entire Report. This was not bluff: I had proposed this radical strategy to both groups earlier. Although both had gulped at its confrontationalism, both accepted my confident assertion that the Socialists would let it pass. They did.

This success enabled me to be chosen as the Parliament's Rapporteur in 2003 on the follow-up Commission White Paper. Following the earlier battle it was much more straightforward this time, though there was a huge amount of work involved over many weeks finessing the final wording through various colleagues. I was very pleased with the end result. Businesses of all sizes called me to say that they were pleased too.

One of Stephen's other UK colleagues is Peter Skinner. Peter understands a great deal about the construction industry, and was keen to put his stamp on a Health and Safety Directive concerned with the use of ladders and scaffolding. Proposals were made that two people should not be on a ladder at the same time, that it should be illegal for someone to stand at the bottom of a ladder and hold it, that people should be trained to climb ladders and that EU funding should be made available for the training. In Tory circles this became known as the 'Rickety Ladders Directive.'

Speaking against these proposals, I confirmed that Health & Safety was an important issue: that was not in question. What was in question was the role of the EU in defining the prescriptive detail of how to secure it. Above all, was the European Parliament concerned with the big issues our constituents cared about, how to deliver a better peace, security, prosperity, environment, and quality of life? Or were we more concerned with whether it should be legal for one person to stand at the bottom of a ladder while another person climbed up it?

Some months later I read a letter to the Times from a correspondent who had just bought a ladder. He was intrigued to find that at one end of it there was a red notice, saying *Stop: this is the last rung.* Perhaps the manufacturer had been reading the Skinner Report.

On one occasion when it was Peter's turn to speak in the plenary debate on the Rickety Ladders Directive, his seat was empty. There was no news as to why he wasn't with us: I hoped that he had not had an accident climbing someone else's ladder. His Socialist colleague Helle Thorning-Schmidt was next on the Speaker's list, and said that Peter had meant to send his apologies. She added that something very important had come up, and she hoped the House would understand that only a personal matter of great and sudden urgency would have kept Peter away, and prevented him from notifying his absence personally in advance.

It was a very loyal performance, somewhat undermined when Peter rushed into the chamber just before the debate ended to state cheerily that the Parliament chauffeur had got stuck in traffic when collecting him from a restaurant in downtown Strasbourg. He was most perplexed when the rest of us started laughing.

Helle has at least two claims to fame. One is that Neil Kinnock is her father-in-law. The other is that she was appointed Rapporteur for the Physical Agents (Vibration) Directive. This was another Health and Safety law, designed to address the growing problem of back pain. The theory was that working with certain machinery for too long involved vibration to the body which caused bad backs. There was no scientific evidence to show any quantifiable link between such vibration and back pain, but that didn't stop Helle from proposing amendments that specified low daily limit values which were frankly absurd. The UK Government confirmed that there was no such evidence, and again asked that there should be no amendments to the proposed Directive by UK MEPs. I told Helle bluntly that she had misread the data, but that didn't faze her at all.

The Commission representative was right behind her, or should I say left behind her. He said that he was delighted with Helle's amendments. They were very much in line with the original Commission suggestions to the Council of Ministers, suggestions that the Council had dared to water down. Clearly, here was a chance for the Commission to show the Council who was the boss. I was amazed at their arrogance, as well as their ignorance.

The official UK Government view was that drivers of industrial vehicles such as tractors, excavators, bulldozers, dumper trucks and forklifts could reach Helle's lower limit after as little as two hours per day. Under Helle's proposals they would then be required by law to stop operating the vehicle, or have four specially-trained drivers for each eight-hour shift. The National Farmers' Union observed that if a tractor driver was limited to two hours per day, a farmer would need at least five drivers for each vehicle to bring in the harvest. The whole idea was laughable – except that Helle was serious.

I was determined to do all I could to stop her proposals dead. I suggested to Tory colleagues that they should rapidly arrange to have a picture of themselves on a tractor, taken by their local press. I supplied each of them with a press release to accompany it. The week before the vote, local papers up and down the land featured the story that UK Labour MEPs were joining other Euro-Socialists to put them out of business.

The effect was that we were indeed able to water her amendments down.

Finally I must mention one of the Committee Vice-Presidents, Christian Democrat Winfried Menrad from Germany. He is a most gentle and gracious professor, who has managed to get the reputation within the Parliament as the expert on Works Councils.

The problem, or at least the problem for me, is that he has a very different vision of what approach is needed in this regard. I found his thinking very left-wing. It was no surprise that his Report on European Works Councils was embraced enthusiastically by the Socialists, though not by me.

After many meetings and much wooing, I managed to persuade him to amend his report in several significant ways. He agreed to change his phrase that Trade Unions play a useful part etc, to Trade Unions CAN play a useful part. Finally he agreed that trade unions should only become employees' representatives if that was the declared wish of the particular employees.

These were crucial changes. In return for these amendments, I promised to vote for his Report at least in committee. We both knew his Report would get through anyway, but I also knew he wanted it to be unanimous. He persuaded the Socialists to support my amendments, and the result was indeed confirmation of how consensus and compromise can work. My amendments all passed.

I then pushed my luck a little by proposing a further amendment in the plenary session of all MEPs. In his Report, the definition of dialogue within a company was discussions between employers and employees' representatives. However, there were some companies where the employees might not wish to have representatives between them and the management. I proposed a revision that the dialogue should be between employers and employees OR their representatives, recognising that employers had the right to communicate with their employees directly. Winfried was not happy, and said he had to abstain. The

Socialists were not at all happy, as this might weaken the power of their trade union paymasters. They voted against. But because I had got Bartho on side the whole EPP/ED Group supported me, as did the Liberal Democrats. This amendment also got through. There was an audible cheer from business colleagues in the balcony.

Winfried was later to accost me at the end of a different debate on the proposed Information and Consultation Directive. He said to me: how could I possibly speak against it when I had won so much in Committee? I asked him what on earth he meant. He replied that he had initially sided with the Socialists, in favour of sanctions being levied on companies that failed to comply with the correct procedures. He said that it was as a direct result of my personal pressure that this plan had been outvoted: it would now be left to Member States to impose proportionate and appropriate sanctions, and even this reduced reference was outside the body of the text and merely in a recital. He saw the outcome as a great success for me

I had only seen it as a failure because sanctions were still mentioned. I was reminded yet again how much I had to learn as a politician.

People back home sometimes ask: 'What have I actually achieved as a typical MEP?' In general I believe I have helped to ensure that the voice of business, the voice of job-creation, has been heard loud and clear. Specifically I can claim that most recent proposals on employment and social legislation now include some amendments from me, which I consider have made such legislation less bad. I certainly played a key role in jamming any early agreement on the proposed Atypical Workers Directive, a proposal that the CBI were convinced could have put 160,000 temps out of work. There have also been my own Reports, notably on CSR plus several specifically on SMEs, as well as activity on a smaller scale in the Environment Committee.

But what gives me the greatest satisfaction is the nickname I have earned from other nationalities. The Germans call me Philip the Fighter. The French label me *Philippe le Contestateur*. Opponents and colleagues all know I'm there.

Meanwhile, the tide of future legislation flows on, and it is largely the UK's own fault. The fact that Tony Blair signed up to the EU Social Chapter means that other Member States are no longer fearful of making themselves more uncompetitive vis-à-vis the UK. The floodgates of more social legislation, jammed firmly shut when John Major secured his opt-out, have now been eagerly re-opened.

I shall continue to expose the antics of Labour MEPs who have welcomed this re-opening, and who actively promote yet more and more legislation as a result. In this respect if in no other, the UK under Tony Blair is indeed leading in Europe. In one speech alone, introducing his Report on EU Health and Safety strategy in 2002, Stephen Hughes called for new EU legislation on Workplace Bullying, a new Directive on Workplace Ergonomics, for strengthening of the Display Screen Equipment Directive and for tightening of the Manual Handling Directive. At the same time he urged a comprehensive extension of the Carcinogenic Agents Directive, and demanded a new Directive laying down minimum standards for the Recognition of Occupational Diseases. The Party of European Socialists supported Stephen unanimously in the plenary session, just as they always did in Committee.

I shall continue to crusade that our Committee betrays its mandate because it does nothing to promote jobs, and so much to destroy them. If we wish to help employees, we should spend more energy in helping their employers succeed.

Officially it is called the Employment Committee. I call it the Unemployment Committee.

Chapter Nine

The Road to Damascus

In addition to specific Committee responsibilities, each MEP is assigned to a delegation to visit and receive visits from another country or group of countries. By developing dialogue and sharing views, such visits hopefully encourage more mutual understanding and progressive meetings of minds.

My chosen delegation covered the so-called Mashreq countries, which included Syria, Jordan, Lebanon, Egypt and the Gulf States. I knew little about any of these countries, which seemed an excellent reason to find out more about them especially as the world spotlight was increasingly focussed on this troubled part of the world. But the timing and nature of any visit to such a region have to be carefully planned, given the simmering local tensions. The Middle East was a cauldron in which real Western politicians were regularly boiled alive. We would later see even Tony Blair stewed in Syria, and Iran rejecting the UK choice of Ambassador because our Prime Minister chose to send Jack Straw as his deputy on an official visit rather than grace the country with a visit himself. If only the Iranians realised how difficult it was to fit new countries into Tony's hectic international tour schedule.

Our visit was repeatedly postponed, but finally fixed for late November 2000. As well as myself, the delegation included:
Michel Dary, a French Socialist, Chairman of our Delegation
Sami Nair, another French Socialist
Alima Boumediene-Thiery, also from France, a Green
Ilda Figuereido, a Communist from Portugal
Jannis Sakellariou, originally Greek but now a German Socialist
John Purvis, a fellow British Conservative

The planned programme was crowded, making clear this was going to be no free holiday. I left home midday Saturday for Jordan, arriving in Amman around midnight.

Sunday 19ᵗʰ November 2000

After a brisk breakfast we were bundled aboard a coach to the Jordanian Parliament for a series of briefing meetings. First was a session with the Chairman of the Foreign Affairs Committee and the Speaker of the House of Representatives.

The Chairman wanted to see much more involvement by the EU as peacemakers in the Middle East. He was clear that peace was unlikely with the USA being the only broker. Given the current uncertainty in US politics, (in Florida, they were still deciding on how to recount the recounts for the Presidency), there was not just a need for a stronger EU role but also an opportunity.

We asked what Jordan thought about the West's continued sanctions on Iraq. He replied that stability in Iraq was important for the stability of the region. But Iraq needed to gain the confidence of its neighbours in the Gulf, and the ball was definitely in Iraq's court.

The Speaker then took over, saying that there should be sanctions on Israel for continuing to flout UN Resolutions: Iraq hadn't obeyed and was being punished accordingly – failure to treat Israel equally just showed the double standards of the West.

Our next meeting, with the Chief of the Royal Court, gave a slightly different perspective. He said that Jordanians had no wish to break off relations with Israel. What would happen to their Palestinian brothers if they did? Israel would close all the bridges. Jordanian humanitarian aid to the Palestinians would be halted.

We went to visit our first refugee camp, at Talbiyyah, to see with our own eyes how EU money was being spent. The first project was the creation of a football field – if a large oblong of red dust could be called a field. Over half the people in the camp were children, and such a play area was much needed.

We looked at several houses that were being upgraded. One was home to a disabled man, his wife and his 11 children. It had just two rooms. There were around a thousand such homes that needed help. There was enough EU money to help 15.

On our return we passed via the home of the EU Ambassador, whose role was to co-ordinate all the EU-funded projects. The indoor swimming pool was all lit up. The views over Amman were stunning. The contrast with the Talbiyyah camp was dramatic.

Today a 14-year-old Palestinian was shot dead by Israeli troops at the Gaza border. He had been throwing stones. The Israeli army closed the Karni crossing between Israel and the Gaza strip, thereby blocking food and basic goods from entering Palestinian territory.

Monday 20th November
Up early to check out and be ready to roll at 9am towards the Syrian border, which we reached an hour later.

Our destination was Dera'a, where our Delegation Chairman was due to open a Community Rehabilitation Centre funded via the ECHO programme. We arrived at the right time, but not exactly in the right place. The local policeman decided that our bus could most sensibly be parked on the right of the local square. The problem was that the reception committee was lined up on the left, and nobody told us they were there. It was only when we were ushered to our seats that I noticed the special welcome party: a column of startlingly dressed children, all with banners ready to wave, being tearfully marshalled back onto their school bus without having welcomed anybody.

I immediately rushed towards them. Their teacher saw me, and swiftly got the children back into line. They waved and sang. They gave V-signs (the right way round, of course). They had welcomed us after all (well, me, anyway). I had made their day, and they had certainly made mine. I sneaked back just in time for the first of many interminable speeches.

Finally we were able to visit the centre itself. It was a revelation. We saw some of the dedicated teachers and medics, giving such loving attention to some very disadvantaged children. I turned around the small video screen on my camera so that the children could see themselves being photographed. They were slow to catch on, but once they did and saw themselves on the screen their delight was a joy to behold.

At the official lunch I sat opposite a Palestinian who maintained that the Israelis were only gathering in Israel in order to be destroyed. It was all ordained apparently. He added that the Koran made clear that the time would come when trees could talk, and that each tree would say to the Arabs: "There is an Israeli behind me: come and kill him." Every variety of tree would be able to talk, except one. It was significant that the Israelis were currently planting millions of that one type of tree throughout the Occupied Territories, purely so that they could hide without being revealed. He was only drinking orange juice, but Syrian oranges are clearly very potent.

We then began the long drive to the capital. The route took us via Bosra, an old Roman amphitheatre and city complex. This is one of the most dramatic and well-preserved sites in the whole of the Middle East. We were the only tourists there.

Finally we reached Damascus, reputedly the oldest continuously inhabited city in the world. But before we could sample it, we had to go via the house of Ambassador for yet another briefing session. The briefing was long and thorough: the drink was short and sweet. Then we were off to another local restaurant, where we were treated to two dervishes in white skirts whirling away for our delectation – and very probably their own.

There were a number of English voices at various tables. I overheard their Palestinian Tour Guide, Mahmoud, describing the next day's schedule as he wouldn't be with them the following day. As a Palestinian he couldn't leave the country. Always keen for an opportunity to liaise with possible constituents I rushed over and asked if there was anyone there from the West Midlands. Needless to say, there were several couples.

I introduced myself and tried to persuade them that I really was there working hard, and not on a jolly. I certainly convinced Mahmoud. He was fully aware of the work the EU was doing in the region, and he gave me a warm and tearful hug.

Today Israeli helicopter gunships fired missiles on targets in Gaza City, in response to a bomb attack on a bus in which two Israelis were killed. Electricity in parts of Gaza was knocked out.

Tuesday 21st November

At 9am we were in the Ministry of Planning. The Minister began with a ritual denunciation of Israel, described as the intransigent occupier. The Syrians had been around for 11,000 years: it was up to others, who had arrived more recently, to seek peaceful co-existence and adapt to the native people of the region.

He then gave some startling statistics. 90% of the factories had less than ten employees. The state had invested virtually nothing between 1981 and 1994, and since 1995 this had even shrunk to zero. They remained hopeful that they could create around half a million new jobs within the next five years. We thought that hopeful was the operative word.

We later learned that 250,000 youngsters join the job market every year, but weak economic growth is only generating 100,000 extra jobs. Youth unemployment is 20% and rising.

We then moved on to a different office, for an audience with the Speaker, President of the People's Assembly. This was essentially a rubber-stamping body, but the Speaker himself was widely respected and an old friend of the former President.

His point was that nobody could prevail upon the ordinary people, the men in the Street, to hide their anger. They had already given up half their land. They wanted action, and they wanted support. They were becoming impatient. We were intrigued that even in an effective dictatorship, the authorities were very concerned about the mood of the Street. There was a clear awareness that demonstrations could turn against the Government if the voice of the people went unheard.

106

We were then escorted to the Foreign Minister. He was one of the strong men of the regime. Unlike previous speakers, he chose to throw the session open to questions straightaway, an action he probably regretted almost immediately. The opening question was from Ms Boumediene, an active campaigner in the European Parliament for Women's rights. She went onto the attack at once: why had Syria such a bad record on human rights, and what was being done to improve them?

There was momentary silence before the Minister retorted in obvious anger. Why was she so concerned about internal Syrian issues? If she was so concerned about human rights, why was she not speaking out loudly against abuse of human rights by Israel? I thought this was a good riposte. She didn't.

I had two questions of my own. One was about the Euro, which Saddam said he would be using instead of the dollar. Did Syria have any thoughts on this? Secondly, if Turkey became a full member of the EU, this would bring the EU boundary to the Syria's doorstep. What impact might that have?

His answers were clear. He didn't believe that Turkey would ever be completely integrated within the EU. The ratio of Muslims in the population, at over 90%, was too high. Regarding the Euro he was at his diplomatic best, saying that he would like to see the Euro play its part in a balanced monetary system in preference to global reliance on the dollar.

In the afternoon there was a gap in the programme so we visited the Old City again. Damascus has a population of around three million: all of them seemed to be in the Old City that afternoon. We walked through the crowded Souk. We strolled along the street called Straight, probably not much unchanged since biblical times. We gazed at the wonderful mosque in awe.

Regrettably John Purvis and I had to cut our visit short. The British Ambassador had kindly invited us for drinks at his home. He gave us a very full and confidential briefing, and a most useful insight into a number of issues. It was reassuring to note that our man on the spot was also on the ball.

On CNN before we arrived we learnt that following the killing of five more Palestinians, Egypt's Ambassador to Israel had been recalled. Today a Palestinian policeman allegedly opened fire on an Israeli motorcyclist on a road inside Israel.

Wednesday 22nd November

An even earlier start today, leaving at 8am for Quneitra, the community at the foot of the Golan Heights destroyed by Israel in the 1967 war because it was alleged to be a base for terrorists. Altogether 244 villages and settlements had been destroyed, and over 150,000 made homeless.

We got on a special UN bus for a tour of the ruins. Nothing had changed since the destruction some 40 years earlier. Israeli settlements were visible in the near distance, separated by minefields, ditches and electric fences. You could tell they were Israeli by the greenness of the irrigated fields, compared to the dry brown of the earth on the Syrian side.

One building was just about intact – though it had no windows and was pockmarked with bullet holes. This had been the hospital.

We could see an Israeli lookout post on the hilltop facing us. We waved. Nobody waved back.

We returned to the UN base for a trip to the Golan heights themselves, via higher and higher check points until we arrived in Shouting Valley. Here families, separated by the 'blue line' which bisects their community, regularly came to shout messages to each other.

When the UN had been invited earlier that summer to go and verify the exact position of the blue line, i.e. the de facto Separation line, they used old GPS equipment that was accurate to 100 metres only. They had no access to satellite photography, and only elderly maps. Each side even used different maps: with the UN using just the official tourist map. Given the sensitivities of border areas, one would have thought the UN would have learnt the importance of mapping with the utmost precision. This was the local UN view too.

We returned wearily to our bus, and ultimately our hotel. Within minutes we were off again, for a special meeting with four intellectuals. They had been part of a group who had daringly signed an open letter complaining about abuses of human rights.

They told us about Palmyra, where 700 political prisoners languished in jail. There was 24-hour surveillance. Light came from a hole in the roof. There was no talking permitted, and no toilet-visits at night. There were many other such concentration camps throughout the country.

For 90 minutes we listened to a series of outpourings from people who knew, from people who cared, from people determined to strive for a better world. We only had one question: what could the EU do to help?

Their answer was simple. They asked for cultural links to be reinforced with the EU, more help for schools, more student exchanges and scholarships, more teaching of European languages – all of this would help open eyes and promote a healthier civil society. We got the message: it was one of many we would be pleased to take back with us.

Walking back afterwards to join our bus we were nearly run over by a speeding car. Next to me on the pavement a complete stranger cried out in English: "He is stupido! You know why? He is Army. You can tell from the numberplate. The Army always drive like that". To say that so openly, in such a closed society, suggests that change in Syria may already be under way.

Today at least two people were killed and 50 injured in a car bomb in Hadera, following the deaths of four Palestinians this morning. Israel blames the Palestinian Authority for letting out so many convicted terrorists, and proudly states that the Israelis are stronger than anyone else in the region, and says "nobody will impose their will upon us."

Thursday 23rd November
Off at 8.30am to head for the Lebanese border.

Our first stop was the old Roman fortress of Baalbek, one of the major wonders of the Middle East, which we had been invited to visit as guests of the Lebanese Government. Except that the invitation had not been notified to the local booking office. So while we left the interpreters and the Ambassador to sort it out, we just gatecrashed and wandered happily over the whole amazing site. By the time we left two hours later, the invitation issue had still not been resolved, so we happily paid ourselves. It was worth it.

When we finally arrived in Beirut we went straight to the local European office for the obligatory briefing session – and another wad of papers to read. We were told that human rights were much more developed here – though this wasn't much help to the Palestinians. They were not allowed Lebanese citizenship, and couldn't vote. They came as refugees, and refugees they stayed.

Discussions continued over a working dinner, where I learned how the political system coped with the religious divide within the country.

Apparently in the Lebanese Parliament there had historically been a 6:5 ratio of Christians: Muslims. The Civil war had changed that, and now there was parity between the two groups. But the Muslims had four sub-groups: the Christians had seven. Each of these sub-groups had to be accounted for pro rata within the overall parity fixed by law. The maintenance of this balance was vital. This was a key reason why the Palestinians couldn't vote: the extra Sunni Muslims would distort the balance.

I think I just about understood the system. I went home to sleep on it, and slept within seconds of hitting the pillow after another exhausting day.

Today Israel shuts down liaison offices in Gaza. Around midnight Israeli planes buzzed Beirut, just to remind Lebanon where the real power lay.

Friday 24ᵗʰ November
Highlight of today's visit was a meeting with the President.

He was very clear that there would be no peace in the region without an overall peace. And just because Israel was a nuclear power did not mean she could do whatever she wanted. In the search for peace, matters were lop-sided because America was not an honest broker. Such a role was wide open for the EU. It was time that the European Union seized the opportunity. We had heard this before, and could not disagree.

Next stop was the Parliament, where we met Members of the Foreign Affairs Committee. John Purvis asked what was their most pressing economic problem. The answer was immediate: Recession, and in the Chairman's eyes it was the fault of the EU. Now this was certainly a new answer. The argument went that Lebanese exports were heavily weighted towards the EU. In return, the EU threw them agricultural goods at heavily subsidised prices, thereby destroying their own Lebanese agricultural economy. Maybe the country should go back to growing opium and hashish as before: was that what the EU really wanted?

Michel talked of the various EU-funded projects in the region. The problems of excess EU bureaucracy became clear. If a tractor needed to be ordered, within the agreed budget for an agreed project, not even the EU Ambassador could give authorisation. It had to go back to Brussels for approval. Brussels was so keen to keep control, for fear of further accusations of mismanagement of funds, that the result was often project paralysis. This had to be sorted in the future. We agreed.

From there we went to the grand French Embassy for a grand French lunch, hosted by the grand French Ambassador. The British Embassy has four diplomats: the French has around sixty, as Lebanon is their entry point into the Middle East. (Despite that, the British Ambassador is the only one always to speak fluent Arabic: it is mandatory for a British holder of the post.)

After lunch we went back to the EU Delegation office for further meetings, including one with Dom Chamoun, President of the National Liberal Party, From there we were driven to the private residence of the new Prime Minister, elected literally only a few days earlier.

He was a millionaire businessman: as a builder and property developer he had been instrumental in rebuilding Beirut, and had also built various palaces for princes in Saudi Arabia. Here was a man who liked making things happen. We had a bracing discussion.

We still hadn't finished our work for the day. Off we went back to the EU Delegation office for a late meeting with the Minister for Displaced Persons. No arrangements had been made for a working dinner so we had to settle for a working banana. The Minister had a tough job. Twenty percent of the resident population of the country was 'displaced', many of them from places that were now firmly part of Israel. Could such people ever be allowed back? Where to? Meanwhile they had no Lebanese citizenship and no official documents. They had nowhere else to go.

Today there were more clashes in the West Bank and Gaza. Three Palestinian protesters were shot dead as fighting raged in the Gaza strip. Uniformed Palestinian security forces opened fire for the first time under a barrage of Israeli fire. A 14-year-old Palestinian was shot near the West Bank town of Jenin, and a 20-year old was shot near Ramallah. An Israeli settler was shot dead in his car.

Saturday 25th November
This morning we visited Chatila Refugee Camp, home of a massacre of 2000 refugees at the height of the Civil War. Ariel Sharon had been Israeli Defence Minister at the time, when the Israeli army surrounded the camp while the massacre took place. The survivors regarded him as a war criminal for allowing it to happen: for them he was an unlikely partner in any future peace.

Our first stop was the local school. It was funded by the UN and had 1000 pupils. They needed a second school, but there were neither funds nor plans to build one. For those who made it to school, there was still no future. 72 professions were forbidden to foreigners (which meant to refugees); such roles included doctors, lawyers, and accountants. Even if they could somehow get a qualification, their qualification could never be used. They had to work as labourers, or running small shops.

They could never break out of their trap.

Not surprisingly drug and alcohol abuse were rife. Occasionally patience snapped and some of the men would leave the camp to attack Israelis. They were usually killed within days: their pictures were displayed in the streets, where they were revered as martyrs. Full-scale war was not seen as an option. But for them the status quo was not an option either.

As we drove out we passed what used to be their recreation ground and football field. It is now the cemetery, for all those killed in the massacre. Today there is nowhere even to play football.

We went back to our hotel for the last time. The late afternoon was free, so I went for a swim in a leisure complex that gave free membership to guests of top hotels nearby. There were four other people in the huge heated swimming pool. Alongside was a separate pool-sized jacuzzi. At one end were special couches, just below water level, with jets of hot water bubbling up. In a corner was a self-contained circular tub where hot water whirled around dervishly at high speed. It was the most sumptuous pool complex I had ever seen anywhere in the world. It was a far cry from the Chatila camp.

Today one more Palestinian was killed in Gaza, with two more killed in different incidents in the West Bank. Hundreds of Palestinians fled their homes as Israeli bulldozers moved in to flatten them.

Sunday 26th November
Up at six o'clock to get to the airport for the flight home.

There was much to ponder. It had been a gruelling week. In terms of hours on the job we had certainly contravened the Working Time Directive. But it had been a most valuable trip. We had realised the value of the EU speaking with one voice operationally on local issues, and in managing local projects. We had established the benefits that simple things such as cultural exchanges could bring. We had appreciated the role the EU needed to play to help the peace. We had met numerous Ambassadors, of different Member States as well as the EU.

But above all we had realised that each of us had been an Ambassador. Despite our lack of experience for such a sensitive role, we felt we had passed the test. We had expressed our concerns to the different Governments. Unusually we had actually listened intently to their own concerns rather than just reflecting ours. We had dared to meddle in the Middle East and had not caused a Third World War. As amateur politicians we felt we had done better than the many professionals.

To confirm this we had some unusual feedback from the Ambassador. Apparently the Syrians had been convinced that Europe and America were both on the side of Israel. The Foreign Minister had originally considered not bothering to meet us. They now appreciated that as representatives of the people rather than Governments, MEPs better understood the Arab perspective. They were delighted and surprised. Our meeting had given them hope.

We all wished we could have done more. There is so much that needs to be done, and the real politicians have been avoiding doing it.

It is so much easier to bomb Iraq.

Chapter Ten

Beefs with France

Before I became an MEP, I thought that the UK was generally the odd man out in Europe. The reality is somewhat different. The country most often out of step is France, dedicated to pursuing her own self-interest.

When the six original Member States came together to found the European Common Market, half of them spoke French: Belgium, France and Luxembourg. The French language, French culture and indeed French interests were very much in the European driving seat, helping to shape both initial policy and the structure of the various institutions. Ever since then the French influence has been under threat, particularly since the UK became a Member – which explains why General de Gaulle tried so hard to keep us out. Anglo-French rivalries run deep.

These differences resurfaced in the early 1990s when BSE was discovered in British beef and dairy herds. The market for UK beef products at home and abroad seized up instantly.

Much work was done in the subsequent years of John Major's government to contain and finally stamp out the disease. Millions of cattle were slaughtered, some of them probably healthy. Rigid and costly control systems were put in place in all UK farms and abattoirs to restore consumer confidence and make clear that food safety was of paramount importance. All of this was done with the full knowledge and support of the EU Commission.

Ultimately the Commission announced that it was satisfied, and that exports were therefore free to resume throughout the EU. It would thus be illegal for any Member State to maintain their own ban on British beef. So just one year into the new Labour government, and conveniently ignoring all the groundwork done by John Major, Tony Blair claimed the credit personally and proudly presented the news as the first direct evidence of his new relationship with Europe: "The beef ban is lifted!"

Except it wasn't.

Most Member States accepted the Commission ruling, albeit with some reluctance, though they still didn't buy any beef. But Germany was wobbly on the issue and France was not happy at all.

The Germans had a particular problem. Following the UK crisis their own domestic market for home-produced beef had collapsed in sympathy. As a major beef-eating nation their farmers were furious, and their government was naturally sensitive to their concerns.

When first signs of their unease hit the headlines, I decided to write personally to all 99 German MEPs, asking them to put pressure on their Government to conform to EU single market rules. It couldn't do any harm, and it might just help a bit, I thought. To my amazement the local press were very excited by such an initiative: the fact that I had apparently written ninety-nine separate letters had really impressed them. It was actually only one letter, sent out 99 times, and it wasn't designed to impress the press but pressure the Germans. Nonetheless I accepted the media congratulation graciously without correction: I was beginning to think like a politician.

There are various arguments put forward as to why France was so intransigent, but certain facts stand out. Before the outbreak of BSE France had been a key market for UK beef. Between 1988 and 1995 our beef exports to France had doubled, topping 100,000 tonnes the year before BSE struck. The UK had become France's major supplier. This was not just for prime beef, but also 'cow-beef' from ex-dairy cows for use in pies and petfood. Once UK beef supply had stopped, French farmers had regained 90% of their domestic market with their own home-produced beef. Farmers have a lot of votes in France. They weren't going to give back the business easily.

In Spring 1999 – or to be exact April 1st, perhaps an appropriate choice of date – France had set up its own Food Standards Agency called AFSSA. Its official mission was to promote food quality and food safety in France. In practice its role was to revisit all the known evidence regarding the outbreak of BSE, and try and come up with a good reason why French beef-farmers should continue to be allowed to protect their home market and keep British beef locked out. That the EU had ruled British beef as safe was regarded as irrelevant. AFSSA was briefed to ask the same questions: the fact that 50% of its governing body was allegedly sponsored by the French agriculture and food distribution industry may explain why it came up with different answers.

AFSSA claimed to have discovered new evidence that the disease was still rife in the UK, that it could still be entering the food chain, and the beef ban should therefore stay in place. The Commission had not done its job properly: thankfully for the health of humankind French scientists had established the real truth.

The Commission was not amused, but responded typically timidly by submitting this so-called new evidence to yet another body specifically set up for the purpose, made up of the most eminent food scientists around. Riskily a Frenchman was asked to chair it. The committee soon established, unanimously, that there was nothing new in the French report, and that British beef was as safe as any beef in Europe. It also confirmed that France was breaking EU law by maintaining the ban.

France took no notice whatsoever. The UK Government, instead of taking a firm line in upholding EU law by referring France to the European Court of Justice without delay, preferred to take a more appeasing line. One must never fall out with one's European friends, even if it means failing to stand up for one's own national interest. For Labour, that is what being at the heart of Europe is apparently all about. So talks were started, which dragged on for weeks getting nowhere.

The EU Commissioner responsible for Public Health and Food Safety was David Byrne. He had been a surprise nomination from Ireland for what was to be a very big job. But he had been confirmed in office by the European Parliament, and in September had made his first appearance before the Environment Committee. He talked in some detail about his vision for the future, his priorities and his plans for the coming year. He made no mention of BSE.

When he had finished I thanked him for describing his plans for the year but asked whether he could share with us his plans for the week. In a few days' time, his committee of experts was due to give its response to the French accusations. It was time firm action was taken to uphold EU law. Wasn't that why he was there?

I got a fairly floundery political answer, which in essence said that he hoped that further discussions might resolve the matter shortly. He was not convincing. As he left the meeting I followed him out and asked him point blank whether MEPs could do anything to help. In the business world, we would always meet such issues head on: I just could not understand why politicians were always pussyfooting about. Certainly our own Government strategy – if that was the appropriate word – seemed to be downplaying the issue, keeping matters cool, and it wasn't getting us anywhere. Surely we needed to raise the temperature and increase the noise level? To my amazement and delight he fully agreed. Anything we could do to increase the noise would help increase his leverage on the French.

My colleague Struan Stevenson MEP suggested we march on Paris.

A few weeks later ten Conservative MEPs took the fast train to Paris and headed for the Arc de Triomphe. We had with us a rolled-up banner, which when unfurled said (in English on one side, French on the other) "Marie Antoinette said Let them eat cake. Conservative MEPs say Let them eat British Beef". It was going to be a great photo-opportunity, so we told a few key press to be there to greet us.

Somehow we seemed to have forgotten to ask permission from the authorities for our demonstration, for the very good reason that such permission just might not be given in case we were riotous. Technically we would be breaking the law, but we were planning to be very well-behaved. After all, we were Conservative politicians.

We arrived at the Arc de Triomphe at the appointed hour, and to the surprise of the two local gendarmes. We unfurled our banner, and chanted our slogan most discreetly. Three of the press had arrived just ahead of us, and the cameras rolled. The gendarmes continued to look on, though one of them did seem to be talking rather rapidly into her radio. Two plain-clothes police arrived. So did more photographers. We said we wished to stroll gently down the Champs Elysée giving out leaflets, so the local police graciously stopped the traffic round the Etoile and we confidently walked across to the safety of the other side. More photographers arrived.

They were suddenly joined by a squad of armed National Guard, which had been specially summoned by radio. Ten Tory MEPs were clearly a major threat to national security. We were surrounded on all sides, unable to move.

At this stage the EU proved its worth. Each one of us produced a diplomatic passport. This is normally a completely useless document, offered to MEPs really as a souvenir. It looks a bit like the old British Passport, and asks all Governments to be especially nice to the Bearer. We were advised never to use it at Passport Control, as officials would wonder what it was and you would get held up while they examined it from cover to cover and showed it to their colleagues. But now it came into its own. We were diplomats. We could not be arrested nor detained against our will.

This was news to the National Guard and to their plain-clothes bosses. There was a barrage of radio conversations between layers of bemused officials trying to work out what to do with us. We were breaking the law, but there was nothing in the handbook on how to deal with demonstrating diplomats. By definition, diplomats didn't do that sort of thing.

In the end we got tired of being stuck, so a few of us decided to push our way through and see what happened. There was a minor scuffle - but then we were through. We had made it clear that we had an appointment with the British Ambassador to discuss the Beef issue in more detail, and had flourished a letter from the Embassy in proof. We were reluctantly allowed to walk on to the Embassy – with our armed guard still in attendance – where we had a very productive meeting.

On the way my mobile phone rang: it was one of the West Midlands radio stations following up on my press release. I was able to give a live interview as I marched along together with our armed guards in my new status as international criminal. It was certainly an unusual broadcast.

When we emerged from the Embassy the police were still there, and so were even more photographers. The police stayed with us until we were finally in taxis heading for the station and our train back to Brussels. I don't think they had enjoyed their day. We had.

The following morning the world enjoyed it too. Our demonstration had been headline news, not just in the European press but across the globe. We had never expected such mass media attention. If the French police hadn't over-reacted we would never have got it.

The reaction back home was equally unbelievable. Wherever we went we were applauded loudly. The *Daily Mail* ran a leading article referring to the new breed of MEPs who were prepared to get off their butts and out into the real world. That had been our approach exactly. We wanted to be where the action was. Where necessary, we would be the action.

In Brussels, I bumped into Labour MEP Simon Murphy who graciously congratulated us on the tremendous campaign coverage. I began to think he might be a genuine guy after all. I was soon to be reminded that he was first and foremost a politician, when he later referred to it in the *Birmingham Post* as a silly stunt. Apparently we should have been doing something more useful, such as talking to each other back in some committee room in the Parliament. His version of events found few takers.

Meanwhile the UK Government persisted in fruitless discussions with the French. In the process, Agriculture Secretary Nick Brown was talked into a remarkable series of concessions, under the guise of a clarification to the French of our UK safety control procedures. Naively he signed up to an even tighter labelling regime specifically to ensure a prompt recall of British beef should a health risk emerge. By so doing, he confirmed to the French press that a health risk might indeed exist.

Despite this major concession to the French, predictably there was still no movement on their part whatever. Given the UK was so eager to do all the conceding, France felt under no pressure to change. It was only at the year-end (1999) that France was finally referred to the European Court. Precious months had been lost. It would not be until December 2001 that the Court would rule – that France had indeed been acting illegally. This decision again the French chose to ignore, while simultaneously battling to have the new European Food Safety Agency located in France so that they could lay down EU law for everyone else to follow.

The UK Government had the usual limp response. It welcomed the judgement and "hoped" that France would observe the European Court ruling.

The irony is that during this period it emerged that some French cattle were being fed, illegally, on sewage sludge. Totally separately, the EU's Food and Veterinary Office (FVO) had visited France in June on a regular inspection visit and had discovered that meat from BSE-infected cattle might still be entering the food chain – in France.

Although meat and bone meal was banned in animal feed back in 1996 in the UK, in France it was still in use. Labelling laws were routinely ignored. Sampling of such feed was done at an insufficiently low level, with some areas not covered at all. Most of the 200,000 fallen cattle each year were not being examined. Inspections within abattoirs were not being carried out in accordance with EU law. Documentation and testing of emergency slaughtered animals was incomplete. The FVO team of experts criticised the entire BSE monitoring and eradication programme in France. But that still didn't stop French beef being freely available for export throughout the EU, or stop our own Government rejecting calls to ban it.

Throughout this episode France had been single-minded in standing up for her own national interest. Conforming to EU law was to take second place, but this was not unusual. France has the rare distinction of being at or near the top of two lists. One is the list of those EU countries that are the worst/slowest in transposing EU Directives into national law, to give them legal force in their own country. France is right there. The other is the list of countries with the most cases pending against them in the European Court for failing to implement EU laws once they have been transposed. France is there too.

I raised this issue in the full session of the Parliament in Strasbourg via a question to the Portuguese Presidency of the Council. France was due to take over the Presidency six months later. I suggested that the Presidency should not rotate automatically among Member States on a Buggins' turn basis. It should only go to countries that showed their commitment to upholding the authority of EU institutions. The Presidency should therefore be confined to countries who did well in a league table: they should be in the top half of Member States in terms of the fewest cases pending against them in the Court; they should also be amongst the best in transposing EU laws. I had no particular country in mind, of course. I was making a very general point. Surely no one could disagree.

Needless to say, my question was not exactly answered, so I tried again with a supplementary question. The following is an extract from the verbatim record:

"Mr President. I note that you said this particular issue was not currently on your agenda for the next IGC (Inter Governmental Council) but if some people wished it you would consider it. Well, I and my fellow 35 British Conservative MEPs wish it and would like you please to consider it. I appreciate that it is a provocative question. It is meant to provoke because there is a very serious issue here that some countries do not hold EU law in the respect which it deserves. We have to find a way of putting pressure on such countries to do just that so we can reconnect with our citizens. I cannot think of a better way to do it. Can you?"

The answer was that they might look at the idea. On the other hand they might not. Indeed they didn't.

The following week I wrote in similar vein to the French Ambassador to the EU asking for his comments, and hopeful of a reply. I am still waiting for it.

I was to return to this subject when the Parliament debated a Report on the role and the site of the proposed new European Food Safety Authority. Various countries put in bids to be host for this prestigious new Agency: the UK Government typically decided not to bother.

I proposed a formal amendment to the legislation, saying that the Agency should only be awarded to a country in the top half of a league table of Member States, in terms of the least cases pending in the European Court of Justice. This Agency was all about upholding EU law, and therefore couldn't sensibly go to a regular flouter of such law.

To my delight, this amendment was passed unanimously in Committee, so I naively assumed that as it was now built in to the body of the Report it would be plain sailing in the full plenary session. But I had been rumbled. The Italians suddenly realised that on that basis their bid for Parma would be excluded. The Spanish realised Barcelona would be out too. And France belatedly realised that their bid for Lille would be a complete non-starter. So French, Spanish and Italian MEPs from all political parties combined together to ask for a separate vote on my new paragraph so they could vote for its deletion. Although the finally tally was 260 votes in favour of keeping it, as opposed to around 213 against, I had failed to secure the necessary 314 votes (for a Second Reading. It had to be half of all MEPs eligible to vote, plus one) to keep it in place. A simple majority was not enough, but a marker had been clearly put down.

Meanwhile, France not only continues to look after its farmers. It looks after its Air Traffic Controllers and Pilots, who are uniquely permitted to speak French in and over France despite English being the sole language permitted for airline traffic everywhere else in the world. It looks after its ski-instructors: somehow non-French ski instructors never manage to pass the local exams. It also protects its food manufacturers, with a little help from selected other nations from time to time.

Since the UK joined the Common Market back in 1973, British Dairy Milk Chocolate had not been allowed to be sold throughout the EU. Eight Member States, Belgium, the Netherlands, Luxembourg, Germany, Spain, Italy and Greece – plus of course France – had combined to outlaw chocolate containing vegetable fat being sold in Europe as 'Chocolate'. The remaining seven countries, including the UK, had been graciously allowed to carry on producing chocolate with up to five per cent vegetable fat for home consumption. But home did not include the other eight countries of the so-called single market. The original 'Cadbury' formula of 20% cocoa solids and 20% milk solids was not deemed to be sufficiently European. Only 25% cocoa solids and 14% milk solids would qualify - which would mean changing the recipe, altering the taste, and most unfortunately reducing the appeal for UK customers. The one and only true continental chocolate had to stay protected from such inferior competition.

In 1996 a so-called compromise proposal was put forward graciously allowing milk chocolate to be sold after all, as long as the name changed to 'vegelate'. This idea was swiftly binned by the British and Irish. The following year another scheme was proposed. Firstly such products should in future be described as milk chocolate with a high milk content. If that appeared to sound harmless, on the continent it was to be blessed with the title 'chocolat de menage', translated as 'household milk chocolate'. Finally, there should be clearly printed on the front of the packet as a sort of health warning: 'Also contains vegetable fats other than cocoa butter.'

These proposals were put forward by France and Belgium, anxious to protect their own domestic markets. They were supported by the Dutch, who imported most of Europe's cocoa into Amsterdam and just happened to have the largest cocoa-grinding industry in the EU. The UK chocolate industry was aghast.

In Strasbourg the vote had been 306 to 112 in favour of these unhelpful proposals. It wasn't just the French and Belgian MEPs who said 'Oui'. The Socialist vote against the British national interest was led by the PES leader, the one and only Pauline Green, Labour MEP for London North.

The Commission fortunately decided that Parliament's amendments were too draconian, so went back to the drawing board. The required solution was not to be harmonisation. It needed to be mutual recognition of the different national chocolate-making traditions amongst Member States. The consumer should be free to choose. That was after all supposed to be what the single market was all about.

Behind the scenes a compromise or 'common position' was thrashed out within the Council of Ministers by qualified majority vote. France and Belgium were still against any compromise, but they no longer had enough votes to block progress: Germany had changed sides. The Germans had belatedly realised that the traditional continental recipe could only produce traditional chocolates. Innovation, which was driving market growth in the UK and elsewhere in the world with 'aerated' products for example, positively required greater use of vegetable fats. It could be good business and they didn't want to miss out.

There would need to be minor recipe adjustments so that everyone could save face. The name would now have to be 'family milk chocolate', which was not objectionable, rather than simply 'milk chocolate'. But it would still be up to the European Parliament to have the final say.

The Parliamentary campaign against the Council compromise began in earnest some weeks earlier. The month before the main vote in the plenary session, the Environment Committee would give its view on the various amendments being put forward. Almost all the amendments harked back to the original debate a few years earlier, and tried to re-instate wording that had been rejected by the Commission before. To help the Committee consider the amendments in a balanced way, the French chocolatiers had a small stand opposite the hemicycle giving away French chocolate. To help make the point, their posters and leaflets condemned the *faux chocolat* or false chocolate which heathen cultures such as our own were trying to infiltrate on to the continent. Only one chocolate was the real thing, and its purity had to be protected – purely for the sake of the consumer of course. The interests of the French chocolatiers were naturally irrelevant.

The Belgian Rapporteur called a press conference. On the platform were half-a-dozen white-coated chocolate manufacturers, complete with chefs' hats, warning of the dire dangers ahead if MEPs voted wrongly. A doctor sat at the end of the platform. He said that the powers of cocoa butter were well known, both for their aphrodisiac qualities as well as for the benefits to the cardio-vascular system. The effects of using other vegetable fats (by definition lower quality) were unknown. There might be a major health risk if British chocolate were to be let loose on unsuspecting consumers.

Although the press conference was supposed to be just for the press, two MEPs seem to find their way in there. I was one. The other was Labour MEP Phillip Whitehead. We both said our piece. This time both Labour and Conservatives were delivering the same message, that it was time to move on. The press seemed to agree.

In Committee, I was asked by our spokesman John Bowis to lead for the UK Conservatives, given my food industry background. It was to be a very exhilarating experience, discussing the issues with other nationalities and other parties, and seeing them progressively coming on side. In the final vote in Committee all but two amendments were thrown out.

But other amendments could be re-submitted for the main plenary session, and indeed they were. The voting this time would be particularly important. We wanted the common position to go through unamended. If any amendment received more than 314 votes the whole Directive would have to go back to the Council of Ministers. Under the rules, Qualified Majority Voting would not apply in such circumstances: all fifteen Member States would need to agree. Any one country, such as France, could then block the legislation on its own. This was clearly the French hope, and indeed the French plan.

The day before the main vote, a full debate took place. The Rapporteur was in good voice, and wasn't going to give up easily. But I was looking forward to my slot in reply. Angela had been doing some research and had found a key fact that was to become the cornerstone of my speech. I was able to point out that the first record of hard chocolate being sold in England was in 1657, when a Frenchman had opened a shop in London. If it was legal for a Frenchman to sell his chocolate in England all those centuries ago, surely three hundred and fifty years later it should be possible for an Englishman, or indeed a national of any EU member state, to sell his chocolate in France. For the first and probably last time in my case, the parliamentary record published the word 'applause' after my speech.

A later speaker got rather carried away. A Mr Martinez referred to our chocolate as being adulterated, contaminated and in effect counterfeit. It was not real chocolate. This was however expected because it came from Britain, the country that fed their cattle on corpses, who had given the world BSE, and who knew so little about food that they ate their meat with jam (i.e. redcurrant jelly with lamb). Passions were clearly running high, especially amongst his fellow countrymen: Mr Martinez was French.

The Rapporteur subsequently asked for the vote to be delayed for a further day: he had plans for another press conference. This time, in addition to a team of white-coated chocolatiers, there was a representative from Mali. He spoke at length about the damage to the Mali economy if the market for cocoa dried up. This would be the inevitable result if the new Chocolate Directive were allowed through unamended. Meanwhile, Phillip Whitehead had cleverly produced a representative from Burkina Faso. Burkina Faso were leading producers of shea nuts, one of the main vegetable fat substitutes for cocoa butter. This economy was in a far weaker state than Mali, and shea nut growth was essential for their future.

Every argument was clearly being used on both sides. The stakes were high. All might ultimately depend on how our group voted, being the largest party.

Within the EPP/ED, viewpoints were looking to be polarised along national lines. One of the Group Vice-Presidents, the vivacious Mme Françoise Grossetête – also French – was finally persuaded that the Group should be allowed a free vote on each amendment. It was going to be impossible to agree a party line that would hold.

But because MEPs were so well house-trained that they were used to following the guidance of the whip, many started to ask how on earth they should vote. On the one hand this was good, as every MEP might potentially be on our side. The bad news was they might be on the other side. The worse news was that the person who sat in the front row and normally had the job of putting her thumb up or down to guide the 233-strong EPP/ED group was none other than Françoise Grossetête. There was every likelihood that she might still raise her thumb to guide in favour of certain amendments, purely to steer her French national colleagues of course.

I was determined not to fail at this stage. I sent an urgent e-mail to our Group Chairman, Hans-Gert Pöttering, suggesting that it would be wrong for any Vice-President to put a thumb up or down. A free vote meant people had to be free to make up their own minds. I placed an identical message, face down, on his desk in the hemicycle. His seat was next to Françoise. I also stood firmly in the gangway just before the vote was due to be called to intercept him as he raced down the stairs. I caught him. He had got the message. I sat down and watched him deliver it.

Françoise was visibly furious, but to her credit she observed the ruling. The voting began immediately. One harmless amendment was passed, but all the others failed to reach the magic number of 314 votes. One particularly dangerous amendment was a mere three votes short of success. It had been a close run thing.

Leading the invasion of Paris, just before our 'arrest'

With sacked EU Commission Chief Accountant, Marta Andreasen

Celebrating the success of the 'Chocolate Directive' with Theresa Villiers MEP

Judging cakes at the Ludlow Food Festival

Yet more eating for England -
Campaigning in Redditch for the farmers

With Charles Tannock MEP at a nuclear power station in Slovakia

The Mashreq delegation, facing Israeli forces on the Golan Heights

Col. Kowalczyk of UNDOF points out the demilitarised zone between Israel and Syria

Inside Chattila refugee camp

The perils of campaigning (1)
Demonstrators outside the house:
'My MEP stands for More Environmental Pollution'

The perils of campaigning (2)
Edward McMillan Scott MEP not knowing where to stand
at the Penistone Show.

The perils of going away:
Angela with a week's post

*Celebrating a joint 60th birthday (above) with Wim Van Velsen
MEP (centre). Hans-Gert Pöttering MEP is on the right.*

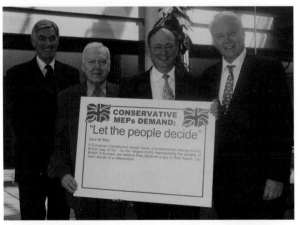

*The West Midlands Conservative MEP team calling for a
referendum on the EU Constitution*

But we were home. At long last British chocolate could be sold throughout the continent. More significantly, it could be sold in France. The French might not yet want our dairy cows, but they could no longer refuse our Dairy Milk.

The above are just some examples of the way France fights its corner. Others deserves a brief mention. Whenever key jobs come up in any EU institution, there is nearly always a French candidate, backed with great determination by the Government of France. For them it is a win/win situation. If the candidate succeeds, fine. If not, then France makes it exceedingly clear that, to be fair, their next candidate should get the next job the next time around. They lose nothing by this process, and on balance they come off better: they secured a French nominee as the next Governor of the European Central Bank as a result, even though he was under investigation for alleged financial fraud at the time.

Opposition to the liberation of Iraq was another example of France standing up for her national interests, in this case her oil interests given the size of the contracts signed up to with the Saddam Hussein regime and now potentially worthless. The statement that France would block any second UN resolution regardless of its content was most revealing. Even more so was the nationality of the first oil company delegation to visit Baghdad once the war was over: Total Elf was allegedly there in strength within 36 hours.

This chapter could be read as a diatribe against the French. If so, I have failed to make the point clearly. My message is the exact opposite. Member States are expected to stand up for their national interest. It is the way the EU works. France fights for France – yet is labelled neither obstructive nor anti-European.

The UK under Tony Blair takes a very different view: "thou must not fall out with friends under any circumstances". This is so inane. In the business world I wanted – and needed – to have friendly relationships with our supermarket customers. But if I was so determined to be friends that I said yes to every demand, I would simply get rolled over like many other suppliers. When I said No, and they knew that I meant it, I retained their full friendship but gained respect on top. I saw, and still see, no reason why politics has to be different.

Clearly French politicians agree with me rather than Tony Blair. Nonetheless, three years after Labour took over the Government the UK Minister for Europe stated that the country had gone along with every single initiative within the EU, and he said it as if he was proud of it. Meekly going with the flow is certainly one option. Putting down constant markers regarding your own national interest is another.

The question is not why France does this so fiercely. The question is why the UK under Tony Blair does not learn from the French

Chapter Eleven

Babel

At the original selection interview at Kidderminster, each of the MEP candidates had been asked about language skills. I said that I spoke some French, a little German and had been fairly fluent in Portuguese when I had run a business in Lisbon, but that had been twenty years earlier. John Corrie said truthfully he only spoke English.

Clearly, it is always a help to know something of other European languages in order to get inside the hearts and minds of the various nationalities. But John had given a very good answer: to be a successful MEP it is not necessary to speak any other language at all other than your own - though it does help if your own language just happens to be English.

In committees, and in the full parliamentary plenary sessions, MEPs are strongly advised to speak their own language, and to leave it to the translators to translate simultaneously. This is not a decree by the translators' trade union. The translators are professionals, and they are more likely to translate better than the amateur linguists amongst the MEPs.

Each day of the plenary sessions, the parliamentary written record publishes the verbatim speeches of the day before in the original languages as spoken. It does look rather odd when the contributions of successive speakers are published in different languages, especially when those present in the Chamber have had them simultaneously translated into their own language.

It also makes for less emotional debates. With the voice of the translator coming through earphones several seconds after the original speaker has sat down, there is not the immediacy, the heat nor the cut and thrust of Westminster. The words can be translated, but not the passion. It can also be disconcerting when a deep bass male speaker is translated by a young female voice.

Translation can give extra spice though if you make a funny comment. As the different translators translate it at different speeds, the laughter can ripple around the Chamber for a long time.

In my maiden speech in Strasbourg I referred to my previous job as Managing Director of a company producing pork scratchings. Although this was only one of our minor product lines, I said that I included a reference in my speech purely to test the translators. They didn't seem to find this particularly funny. The English sense of humour is always a challenge.

The translators take their job very seriously. It is a big responsibility. A member of the translation services sits in on every committee meeting in case there is a query or complaint about a translation into one particular language. There quite often is.

The problem is compounded by the fact that some identical words have different meanings in different languages. The most notable example of this is the famous 'F' word, Federalism.

To the British, Federalism means a superstate, with all powers wielded by one single central authority. To the French and Germans in particular it means the opposite: it means subsidiarity, i.e. decisions being taken as close as possible to the issue and as far away from central diktat as possible. It is all potentially most confusing. We certainly need the translators.

Sometimes the challenge may be beyond them. I recall a debate in the environment committee when it was revealed that French farmers had been feeding their cattle on sewage sludge. Committee Chairman Caroline Jackson challenged the Commission on this, and afterwards said it was clearly difficult 'to flush out an answer on sewage'. The English speakers thought the pun very funny. The translators didn't manage to pass on the joke.

When I hosted a meeting in the European Parliament of the European Cider and Fruit Wine Industry at the suggestion of Bulmers, I concluded my welcome speech with my favourite limerick:

> *There was an old lady from Ryde*
> *Who ate a green apple and died.*
> *The apple fermented*
> *Inside the lamented*
> *And made cider inside her inside.*

The translators had wisely taken the evening off.

I still recall the day in Committee when a German talked of proposals for a tax on champagne. The German word for champagne is Zekt, and in German he spoke of a Zekt-tax. The English translators misheard it and referred to it as a sex tax, which caused great confusion as well as hilarity.

There are currently 11 official languages in the fifteen Member States: Ireland and the UK both use English; Austria joins Germany in using German; Luxembourg and Belgium both use French – but then Belgium has Flemish as an official language as well. Not only do documents have to be translated into all these languages after hours: so do speeches by a small army of interpreters on the spot in real time.

Around 6,000 of the Commission staff are translators or interpreters. Individually they can earn from around €35,000 p.a. for the most junior to around €100,000 for the most senior. Every year there are 1.3 million pages of documents that need translating, and 11,000 official meetings in need of simultaneous verbatim translation. There are very few people who can do such a job at the skill level required. Not only do they have to sustain manic concentration, to be able to listen in one language and translate simultaneously into another. They also have to be able to do this in at least four languages each.

Back in the Parliament, in the key committee rooms and in the hemicycle, the 11 interpreters' booths generally each contain three interpreters. Between them they have to cover all eleven languages.

The good news is that understandably they tire easily. They can only do $3^1/_2$ hours at a stretch for committee meetings. It is a splendid way of ensuring that committee meetings always end on time.

None of the above is an argument for Brits not to bother about learning other languages. A number of us have been having language lessons in Brussels, paid by the EU. Some have also taken advantage of a special facility offered by the Parliament for language lessons in another country during the holidays.

The Parliament will pay for the lessons in full if they are taken in an approved language school, will re-imburse the actual cost of travel to the appropriate country, and will also pay half a personal daily allowance as well. That may sound like a canny way to subsidise a holiday, but a minimum of four hours a day of one-to-one intensive teaching is hardly a holiday. Such a method though certainly helps develop language skills rapidly (it is how I learnt Portuguese originally), and I finally availed myself of this opportunity on a visit to Italy in Spring 2002. At the same time I paid for Angela to have lessons in Italian cooking and Art – not that I felt she needed lessons in either.

But even then, bureaucratic rigidities came into play. The system dictated that Parliament would only pay for me if I had 20 lessons over a period of five successive days, which is what I booked. But the school came back to me and said Wednesday of that week was May 1st and would be a holiday, so no lessons that day. No problem I thought: I would simply allocate the missing four lessons over the remaining four days. The Parliament secretariat said this was outside the rules, which were very clear. Five days meant five days. Finally, after a lot of fuss, mutual honour was satisfied when I got a receipt from the Language School correctly if misleadingly saying that I had received the full 20 lessons over the period of five days 29th April - 3rd May. This had been all very tiresome, but another small battle won against the bureaucrats felt really good.

Learning Italian felt really good too, though even at the end of the course I realised how much I still had to learn. I was showing off my new-found skills to my teacher by describing in what I hoped was Italian some of the differences between our two countries. I said that in England bread was regarded as fresh even if it was many days old: this was possible because our bread was filled with preservatives. I invented the word *preservativi* which I thought should be ok. My teacher was most intrigued as to why English bread should be filled with contraceptives.

In the lift in my apartment block in Brussels there is a printed notice saying: 'Not to be used by childrens behind fourteen years'. In many local hotels one can be confident of finding the invitation to guests: "for comments, please also write on the backside". Perhaps I am not the only one who could benefit from further language tuition.

Whenever I visit schools back in the UK, I stress the importance of students learning a second language – and to regard it as a second language rather than a foreign one. Foreignness implies distance. I also remind them of a statement by former German Chancellor Willy Brandt: "If you want to buy from us, it is fine to speak English. But if you want to sell to us, *dann mussen Sie Deutsch sprechen.*"

Germany has nonetheless been realistic about the growing importance of English. In Spring 2000 the country's largest state, North Rhine - Westphalia changed the school curriculum. In future, children as young as eight would get at least two hours of English teaching a week. Previously, no languages had generally been taught until the children were eleven. Other German States are expected to follow suit.

If the Germans are relaxed about the general onward march of English, the French are not at all amused. Their Académie Française makes regular forlorn attempts to weed out English words from the French vocabulary: despite their efforts, le week-end and le marketing manager are both here to stay. The French Government tries to limit by law the number of American films on French television, and insist on dubbing into French those that do get through.

France also accuses the English-speaking Italian Commission President of galloping anglophilism, assuming that this is the correct translation of *l'anglophilie galopante*. Where are the official translators when you need them? On the subject of Commission spokesmen, a Swiss journalist said that before Prodi's arrival all official communications were generally in French, with some English footnotes. Since Prodi, the two language roles had been inverted. The Prodi Commission is the first Commissariat in history where the majority of Commissioners voted to choose English as their main working language. It is a long way since 1995, before which time France contrived to ensure that English was never allowed to be used in Commission Press Conferences.

When the first EU candidate countries came to Brussels for the launch of accession talks, only two of them spoke in French. The other nine addressed the Commission in English. They then submitted their formal written applications in English as well. It was no surprise that the French had a clear view about this, but the writing is on the wall and the writing is inexorably moving to English.

Roughly 60% of all EU documents are currently first drafted in English. 60% of the world's broadcasts are already in English (well, American). 70% of the world's mail is addressed in English. 80% of all data stored on computers is English. 85% of all the world's scientific papers are published in English. One language is used by all the world's airline pilots (except the French). And when the European Central Bank, meeting in Frankfurt, decided they only wanted one official working language, they chose English and not German.

But this disguises a much more fundamental problem. How will the EU cope when all the candidate countries have joined, and when all want to speak their own individual languages? The answer is: with great difficulty.

It was written into the original Treaty of Rome that people throughout Europe should be able to ask a question, and receive an answer, in their own language. This ruling has been applied with some discretion: for example, 'minor' European languages are not recognised as languages for this purpose.

It is not generally known that there are more than a dozen minority languages living and lurking in different parts of the EU:
- Basque, Catalan and Occitan in Spain
- Breton in France
- Corsican in Corsica
- Frisian in the Netherlands
- Friulan and Sard (or Sardinian) in Italy
- Gaelic in Ireland and Scotland
- Ladin and Sorbian (yes, not Serbian) in Germany
- Lapp in Finland and Sweden (Lapland)
- Luxembourgish in guess where?
and of course Welsh in Wales

These have notional protection as a result of the setting up in 1982 of the European Bureau of Lesser Used Languages, rejoicing in the acronym of EBLUL which sounds like an obscure language in itself. This was cemented by the European Charter for Regional or Minority languages, ratified by the UK in 2001. The EU can always be relied upon to have a charter, as well as a bureau, even for lesser-used things.

But this has created other problems. With enlargement approaching the Minister for Culture for the Government of Catalonia wrote round to all MEPs. His point was that Catalan was spoken by 7,187,303 people and understood by 9,844,805. He had obviously been very busy counting. His proposition therefore was that as Catalan was more widely used than at least six of the languages spoken by candidate countries, and indeed more widely used than Finnish or Danish within the present EU membership, Catalan should be promoted to the status of an official EU language with its own interpretation. Logically it would be a fair conclusion. Practically it would just make the translation worse, and we have enough problems as it is. The Minister's success in ensuring that all Harry Potter films are to be dubbed into Catalan shows that the cause is taken seriously, at least by some.

Others have also been active. In Autumn 2002 the UK Government was persuaded that Kernuak (Cornish), one of the Brythonic branch of Celtic languages and spoken at times by very nearly fifty people, should also become officially recognised. After a two-year inquiry, Local Government Minister Nick Raynsford said that the Government now recognised Cornish as the UK's sixth official minority language alongside Lallans Scots and Ulster Scots. This would be at a level below Welsh, Irish Gaelic and Scottish Gaelic but would still qualify for millions of pounds in lottery funding.

Unsurprisingly the 150-member Northumbrian Language Society is now claiming similar recognition.

With lottery money so liberally available I am surprised that the Black Country is currently silent on this matter. Having worked there for eight years I can vouch that they have a language all their own. I well recall going round the Wednesbury snacks factory very early one morning during the night shift with the Red Mill Operations Director Colin Pope.

One of the Team Leaders said: "We am knackered".

Colin, happily a fluent Black Country speaker, was able to respond immediately: "So am we".

With 11 official EU languages at the moment there are 110 (11 x 10) possible translation combinations (speakers of 11 different languages each needing to be translated into the other ten).

The ten candidate countries expected to join in 2004 will bring at least nine new languages: Polish, Hungarian, Estonian, Czech, Slovak, Slovenian, Latvian, Lithuanian and Maltese - always assuming Cyprus just uses Greek. An extra nine languages may not sound much, but it raises the total combinations to 380 (20 x 19). Romanian and Bulgarian may follow. Doubling the membership quadruples the language problem – and doesn't even allow for the possible inclusion of Turkish. With extra interpreters plus support staff, there will be an increase of some 2,500 civil servants. Given the need to uprate computers and libraries, the total cost will be in the hundreds of millions of Euros.

Latvia may even pose an additional challenge. In 2002 it was finally recognised in the Latvian constitution that the Russian language, spoken by 40% of the inhabitants, should enjoy equal status with Latvian. This news has not yet filtered through to the EU interpreters.

Currently in each committee and plenary session a team of 33 interpreters is required: three interpreters in each of the 11 language booths just manage to cope. With 20 languages there would need to be at least 100 interpreters, with five in each of 20 language booths. Meanwhile the Parliament's language booths only have room for three people: there is just very little space to expand their size let alone their number.

There is another problem too: a chronic shortage of interpreters who can speak at least four languages each, including at least one of the candidate languages. Even now, interpreters speaking some pairs of languages simply do not exist. The problem is compounded by the fact that the present list of Indo-European languages will be joined by two Slav tongues, by the Finno-Ungrian languages of Estonia and Hungary, and by a form of Arabic when Malta joins. These are heady combinations for interpreters.

One logical answer might be that everyone should speak English. There are regular letters in local UK newspapers pointing up the absurdity of using so many languages within the EU, and asserting that English is the obvious answer. These same authors are usually the champions of subsidiarity. If the chosen single language were to be French, they would be the first to point out the iniquity of a central superstate dictating that separate national languages were being outlawed. A single language is not yet possible for all official business.

The options are however very limited, unless there is a radical change in approach. But change is not foreseen in the founding Treaty. The requirement to speak and hear in your own language is set in Roman stone.

The Council of Europe, with over 40 members, has only two working languages: English and French. So does the International Olympic Committee. The United Nations, with over 180 members, works in only six languages. (NATO manages with only one official language, namely English, which perhaps partly explains why the French dislike it so much.) The EU, with the prospect of a mere 25 members, should in theory be able to find the flexibility to cope. But flexibility has never been the EU's strongest point.

It is not just in the Parliament that multi-lingualism is a problem. Inventors throughout the EU have clamoured for a single European patent valid in all EU countries. Currently they have to suffer the cost, time and effort of fifteen separate applications. The EU Commission proposed a formula to achieve this, suggesting that filing in English, French and German should be the order of the day. Spain, Portugal and Greece protested that all 11 languages should be used, with the candidate countries being added in due course to make the problem worse. The Belgian Presidency then proposed that patent applicants could choose between English, French and German while retaining the right to have a full version in their mother tongue. The Belgians said this would reduce the language cost of new European patents from €14,500 to €3,000 at a stroke. But the French and Germans rejected this, as they said if applicants had a free choice they would just choose English.

Only in 2003 was a compromise struck: the initial summary pages must be in all languages but the body of the application can be in just one.

The language issue is but the latest to show how the EU can be paralysed at the prospect of change, how the failure to revisit first principles can lead to imperfect solutions that are costly, complicated and still take time and energy to secure. That is the real moral of this chapter.

Any business, needing to flex to meet market conditions, knows that in a changing world 'No Change' is never an option. The EU has yet to learn this most obvious of lessons.

Chapter Twelve

Fraud and Corruption

The popular view in the UK is that the European Commission is riddled with fraud and corruption. The popular view is not so wrong.

The original problem came to light in 1990, following persistent detective work by the UK Conservative MEP Edward McMillan-Scott. He discovered fraud in the Commission's Tourism unit, with evidence that large grants were being awarded in return for bribes to Commission officials. He reported this to the Commission President Jacques Delors, together with the EU Court of Auditors. He also persuaded the European Parliament's own Budget Control committee to examine the charges more fully. Over the next five years various bland papers emerged from the various EU institutions, but it slowly became clear that nobody was going to take the matter further.

Except Edward.

In February 1995, sick of being fobbed off, he made a formal complaint to the Belgian Fraud Squad. It still took until November 1996 before the Commission finally admitted that there had indeed been "large payments to members of Commission staff, in return for the award of grants".

The 'large' figure turned out to be £3.5 million, according to an internal audit report finally published in July 1998, a mere eight years after the initial allegation.

But this was not the end of the story. One year on and the Belgian police had still not completed their investigations, having been hampered at every stage by an apparent Commission cover-up: this included a refusal to lift the diplomatic immunity of two former Director-Generals until October 1997, thereby preventing police from taking evidence.

Three people were directly implicated in the corruption charges. A temporary official from France had his contract cancelled following an inquiry that named him as allegedly one of those involved in the fraud. He received a pay-off of between £80,000 and £100,000, made up of six weeks' salary for each year of service. Officials said later that without a conviction they were contractually bound to make such a severance payment. By 1999, none of the accused had even faced trial.

A £3.5 million fraud may seem tiny in the context of the overall EU budget, but it became progressively clear that this was just the tip of a very large iceberg. The cost of the various irregularities subsequently exposed could well total as much as £6 billion.

In March 1998, the EU's 1996 accounts were due to be presented to the European Parliament for approval. Agreement of the budget was one of the early powers given to MEPs, and this time around certain MEPs were determined to use those powers to the full. Another UK Conservative MEP, James Elles, then moved onto centre-stage as budgets spokesman. He led the charge to oppose the signing off of the accounts, getting the majority of MEPs to support him. In November 1998, he highlighted the apparent lack of responsibility anywhere within the Commission itself, and proposed detailed reform. The Party of European Socialists, at the time the dominant party in the Parliament, predictably disagreed and rallied behind the Socialist Commission: both were soon to be overtaken by events.

For the following month, the fun really started. An Internal Auditor for the Commission, Paul van Buitenen, 'blew the whistle' and issued a 34-page dossier with evidence of fraud, of failures and of cover-ups. He was promptly suspended on half-pay by the Commission for alleged breach of contract. He had been allowed to tell his bosses – which he had – but to tell the elected Parliament was absolutely not acceptable.

But his story was out, and it was dynamite. He referred to the original tourism case, accusing the Commission of failing to co-operate with the police and never making any serious effort to supply them with sufficient information to permit them to pursue their investigations. But there were so many other irregularities, which collectively read like the latest casebook of Sherlock Holmes.

There was <u>The Case of the Flaming Flax</u>. As early as 1970 there were EU Council regulations prescribing subsidies for growing fibre flax. Because the EU doesn't really have the right climate to produce the right quality flax, there is no market for the poor quality European stuff. Instead of encouraging farmers to switch to a crop they could sell, the EU solution was to give them a subsidy to compensate them for the fact that they couldn't sell it. The aid per hectare was €337 in 1992, but this was steadily raised to €816 in 1995.

As the subsidies grew, so did the flax. What followed illustrates the idiocy of the socialist subsidy mentality. In 1993 Spain had only 187 hectares of flax under cultivation. By 1998, this had jumped to 92,200 hectares. Spanish farmers knew a good deal when they saw one.

In July 1998 a team from the Directorate-General (D-G) for Agriculture and from UCLAF visited Spain to take a closer look. UCLAF is the *Unite de Co-ordination de la Lutte AntiFraude*, in other words the EU Fraudbusters. They concluded that all this flax was being grown entirely for the purpose of collecting the subsidy, because once it was harvested the entire crop was destroyed as nobody had any use for it.

The Spanish Authorities however found only one single case of irregularity. Meanwhile, as the Fraud Squad prepared to move in, much of the flax was 'accidentally' destroyed. Arsonists struck key warehouses, and the flax literally went up in flames. Nobody was ever caught, and nobody can now establish how much flax there ever really was in the first place.

The Spanish Authorities are still looking into the matter. Meanwhile the subsidy is still helpfully available for future flax-growers.

The Case of the Irish-Polish Butter had a number of interesting features. The EU offered a subsidy for butter production, which encouraged excess butter to be produced. The main beneficiaries (apart from the butter-producers) were countries outside the EU who could buy the butter cheaply: such butter couldn't be sold within the EU because there was so much of it that it would cause prices to fall. Under the Common Agricultural Policy that would be the ultimate sin.

Back in 1991 a large consignment of butter was due to go the USSR as food aid. It never arrived. It was last seen being sold in Poland. It later appeared that this was an operation conceived with fraudulent intent right from the very beginning.

An anonymous letter fingered a French company by the name of Fléchard as allegedly being involved. UCLAF looked into it and fined the company €17.6 million.

The French Ministries of Agriculture and Finance asked the EU Commission if the fine could be reduced for this poor French company. Thanks to the intervention of the cabinet of Commission President Jacques Delors – who just happened to be a Frenchman – and the fine was slashed by some 80% to a mere €3 million.

The EU Court of Auditors was unable to establish any proper grounds to justify such a reduction. Their work was not helped by the fact that minutes of the decisive meeting in the private office of Jacques Delors somehow disappeared.

Only in July 2000 did the police finally move in, carrying out more than 70 raids in France and Italy and arresting 30 people. The targets were a number of companies in and around Naples that turned out to be controlled by the Camorra Mafia. These had been the beneficiaries of some £15 million in subsidies over many years.

Meanwhile, a number of the Commission officials responsible for supervising the budget at the time of the original fraud continued to occupy senior positions.

The Case of the Echo Submarines concerned a different budget, the European Communities Humanitarian Office aid budget known as ECHO. Between 1993 and 1995 up to €550 million could not be accounted for. Actual fraud was confirmed as a mere €2.4 million, with the rest blithely put down to poor bookkeeping.

UCLAF began an investigation in spring 1997, when it became apparent that aid funds due for refugees from the genocide in Rwanda and Burundi had been diverted in order to employ additional staff in Brussels. Such staff were known as 'submarines' because they existed below the surface, and nobody really knew they were there. This case involved four fictitious service contracts, with the relevant documentation being forged.

The Commissioner with overall responsibility for the ECHO programme was told about the extra staff being employed not in accordance with regulations. There is no suggestion that he was aware of any fraud, and there is every suggestion that he gave written instructions to the contrary. His instructions were quite simply ignored, and carried on being ignored for many years afterwards.

UCLAF gave a full report back in May 1998, naming various officials including the Authorising Officer, i.e. the official responsible for authorising the fraudulent contracts in the first place. The following month an internal investigation was set up, under the thoughtful control of none other than the Authorising Officer.

UCLAF originally concluded that the contracts were known to be fake when they were authorised. They also produced evidence that duplicate payments were made for the same services to the same people, again with the full knowledge of the officials concerned. More and more irregularities progressively emerged. For example, money was recorded as officially going to an EU-funded land registry office in Sarajevo; it was only some years later it was discovered that no money whatever was arriving – for the very good reason that the land registry did not exist.

The Commission subsequently admitted that documents relating to 2000 separate contracts seemed to have been destroyed. Often though there seemed to have been no documents in the first place. An internal audit revealed that over £1 billion had been handed out to so-called Aid Agencies without any receipts being given, or indeed even asked for. Only one lowly official was dismissed.

The EU Commissioner now in charge of Reform, Neil Kinnock, has been looking into the matter.

Meanwhile, <u>The Case of the Missing Med Millions</u> is still unresolved. The MED programmes are designed to promote co-operation between various Mediterranean regions. Schemes include business/college partnerships, town twinnings etc., with an annual budget of some €60 million per year.

€10 million has gone missing.

Although there was supposed to be a wide variety of programmes, one single interlocking network of companies managed to grab control of most of it. This was allowed by Commission officials even though the result was over-invoicing and a lack of supporting documents for much of the expenditure. It took nearly two years after the Court of Auditors said there were problems to set up an administrative enquiry.

Parliament proposed to the Commission that the whole affair should be put in the hands of the appropriate national authorities in France, Belgium and Italy. Nothing happened. The Commission passed on a few bits and pieces of information, but kept back many of the key files. It is hard to avoid the conclusion that Commission officials were still trying to cover up, to protect colleagues from possible criminal prosecution.

Some key authority is probably looking into this most vigorously, without doubt.

<u>The Case of the Emerging Entrepreneurs</u> was arguably a great success, though hardly in the way intended.

A special European Development Fund had been set up to help emerging nations to become more self-reliant and to boost entrepreneurship. Between 1992 and 1997, the Ivory Coast was sent €73 million.

The EU happily doled out money in each of the five years without hesitation. It was only afterwards, in June 1999 and well after the programme had finished, that it turned out that over a third of the funds had been embezzled. As usual, it was the press that found out first. As usual, the Commission did not exactly rush to advise either UCLAF, or the Court of Auditors, or the European Parliament. As usual, the Commission tried to pin all the blame on the national Government, rather than accept any responsibility for its own lack of control systems.

The irony was that some fraud was very creative. One company operated six different identities from a single address, telephone and fax. Another charged €2000 for baby weighing scales, 64 times the normal price.

At the end of the five-years, a programme designed to encourage budding entrepreneurs, entrepreneurship was clearly flourishing.

My favourite is <u>The Case of the Disappearing Dentist.</u> The Commissioner who had the most accusations levelled at her was Edith Cresson. She had been France's first female Prime Minister in 1991/2, and lasted for a whole 321 days before being fired by President Mitterrand. Since 1983 she had also been Mayor of Chatellerault, a small town near Tours, and retained this role even when appointed Commissioner for Education, Research, Science and Development. Apparently she did not consider this role needed her full-time attention. She was later to be famous for other views too: she claimed that all British men must be homosexual because they failed to look at her lustfully when she walked the London streets.

Anyway, to assist her in her part-time Commissioner job, she clearly needed a scientific adviser specifically to conduct a study into Aids research. She decided that only one candidate would do, even though his previous experience in Aids research was allegedly non-existent. She chose her favourite dentist, Pierre Berthelot.

He was indeed a very close friend, a 'proche', who had boasted publicly that he had drawn up her horoscope. It probably foretold she would shortly recruit her dentist. Anyway, for two years he drew nearly £46,000 salary for doing whatever he was doing. He certainly often felt the need to stay with the Commissioner at her home in Brussels in order to do it. But what he was doing was never very visible. Indeed he himself was never visible either.

During his time 'in office' he produced ten brief 'reports', and went on eighteen separate missions. It just so happened that thirteen of these missions were to his home town of Chatellerault, where the Mayor was still the one and only Edith Cresson.

When the Committee of Wise Men later drew up their report (of which more anon), they branded Berthelot's work as 'manifestly inadequate, in quantity, quality and relevance'. They also labelled his position on the Commission payroll as a 'clear case of favouritism'. Madame Cresson insisted that it was better to hire people you knew than people you didn't know, and that she had done no wrong. The same applied to all the other 'proches' who were also revealed as working for her private office.

Meanwhile, she had a few other problems. Her principal programme that promoted adult education schemes was called LEONARDO. (Every programme in the EU has to have its own acronym.) Essentially it was concerned with vocational and language training to help employment throughout Central and Eastern Europe as well as the EU. It had a huge annual budget of some €600 million.

With such a large remit, and such a hefty budget to match, this took a lot of controlling. So her department appointed a Brussels-based company, Agenor S.A. to do the work. Serious questions were soon to be raised about irregularities, together with allegations of favouritism both in the awarding of contracts and the recruitment of staff. A confidential report suggested that the 'minimum action would be the replacement of the Director and a radical improvement of the management'. It also recommended that Madame Cresson 'seriously considers the continuation of the contract with Agenor'.

Madame Cresson considered very seriously and thought otherwise. Nothing was broken: there was therefore nothing to be fixed. She was in charge and therefore naturally all was well. Parliament was soon to show it took a different view.

The final irony was <u>The Case of the Feeble Fraudbusters</u>. UCLAF, the Commission's front line of attack against fraud within the Commission itself, was on the receiving end of one of the most damning reports ever written by the EU Court of Auditors. It turned out that most UCLAF officials had never been properly vetted, and that their management systems were a joke. Documents were put into folders at random, and as most of them were undated it was impossible to find out later which document referred to which case. There was no suggestion of fraud within UCLAF. But with the whole organisation in such obvious chaos it was really rather difficult to be sure.

There were scores of other cases. The Commissioners immediately concerned didn't regard themselves as responsible. The new President of the Commission Jacques Santer tried to downplay it all, and invited Parliament to back him or sack him. Increasingly MEPs warmed to the latter option.

From the earliest days, the Parliament had the power to reject or propose modifications to the annual budget, as well as to ensure that the Commission administered it correctly. It could confirm (or not) the President of the Commission. One power it did not have, though it campaigned hard for it to be included in the Treaty of Amsterdam, was to censure or sack individual Commissioners. But it could censure the complete Commission if it thought fit.

Given that the Commission anyway technically acted together as a college, then legally it <u>was</u> the whole Commission responsible if anything went wrong: one out, all out. By early 1999 this so-called 'nuclear option' was being seriously discussed, and it looked as if everything would be finalised one way or another in the final months of that five-year Parliament by the old MEPs, well before the new lot arrived.

The cleanest decision would have been for the Commissioners most obviously under the cosh to have stepped down quietly of their own accord. They were not impressed with the suggestion. The EPP Group, supported by the Liberals and the Greens, tried to censure both of them formally, but the French and the Italians, plus Socialists from other countries, voted the proposal down.

The then Leader of the Party of European Socialists (PES), Pauline Green, accused the Tories of being politically motivated because five out of the six Commissioners named were Socialists. She also tried to downplay the evidence of Paul van Buitenen by suggesting that he might be an activist within the Green Party, a party that was clearly committed to condemn the Commission whatever they did.

It soon became clear that if anyone was playing politics it was Pauline Green. She did not want the Socialist Commission to fall. Her original bright idea was to propose a censure motion on the whole Commission so that the Socialists could vote against it. This would show the Commission the support it apparently so richly deserved.

This idea was finally withdrawn in favour of a different resolution which called for a Group of Wise Men (Wise Women were apparently not available) to produce an enquiry into the various allegations within the following eight weeks. This carried easily.

But if the PES thought that the traditional Socialist solution to any scandal, of setting up a task force to look into it, would thereby defuse the issue, they were soon to learn otherwise.

A separate motion proposed a Vote of Censure on the Commission as a whole anyway. It was supported by a massive 232 MEPs. Although 293 MEPs voted against, the 44% vote in favour was a severe jolt for Santer. It was an early-warning sign that Parliament had had enough. Nonetheless the Commission was off the immediate hook, mainly thanks to the Socialists, and the world press the following day had a photograph of Commissioner Neil Kinnock kissing the hand of the lady responsible for the let-off, the PES Leader and UK Labour MEP Pauline Green.

Meanwhile our own Prime Minister continued to preach the need for EU reform whenever he could get a headline in the UK press. It later turned out that never once had Tony Blair even mentioned the fraud issue in the Council of Ministers, and in practice his Labour MEPs in the European Parliament were consistently voting to do absolutely nothing about it. I wondered why – as I have regularly wondered since – why the UK press never highlighted this Government failure.

Meanwhile the Wise Men were at work. Their brief was to 'examine the way the Commission detects and deals with fraud, mismanagement and nepotism, including a fundamental review of Commission practices in the awarding of all financial contracts'.

But how should they deal with the press in the meantime? Thoughtfully the Commission's own media service had briefed them on the subject. They were encouraged to display a measure of 'hypocrisy' and evasion when dealing with the various media. They were told not to get carried away by the quaint notion of 'transparency'. The helpful hints continued: 'It is necessary to learn how to conceal aspects of information…which could give rise to a bad interpretation'. These words of wisdom were allegedly penned by the spokesman for Commissioner Edith Cresson.

The Wise Men's report came out on time in March 1999. It was damning.

Although there was no evidence that any individual Commissioner had personally benefited from any misappropriation of EU funds, there were indeed occasions 'where Commissioners or the Commission as a whole bear responsibility for instances of fraud, irregularities or mismanagement in their services or areas of special responsibility'"

Jacques Santer, Manual Marin and Edith Cresson all got a special mention. Two other Commissioners were criticised for nepotism. A list of detailed findings followed. No further stalling was possible: the whole Commission resigned immediately.

The following day, Jacques Santer – now technically ex-President – issued a statement to the press. It included the following paragraph: 'I note that on the basis of a tiny number of cases of fraud and malfunctioning, which did indeed merit criticism, the Committee's report paints a picture of total absence of responsibility on the part of the institution and its officials. This picture is distorted. I consider the tone of the report's conclusions to be wholly unjustified.'

Defiant to the last, he went on to say that he personally was whiter than white.

But the entire Commission had gone – except that they were somehow still there. There was no provision in the Treaties on how to live without a Commission, even if it was incompetent. So within a matter of moments Jacques Santer moved from President to ex-President to Acting President, a position he would hold for the next four months until the new Parliament met in late July. Until then, the entire squad of ex-Commissioners therefore became Acting Commissioners alongside him. So it was business as usual after all.

It would be up to the new Parliament to deal with the issue, though we would not have any say in the Commissioners' severance package. This was bound to be generous, thanks to the Socialists. Because they had been allowed to resign rather than be sacked, they would each get a substantial golden handshake when they finally stood down. This would be worth two-thirds salary for the next three years. This was not a bad deal for a team that was supposed to have left in disgrace.

One of the first tasks of the new crop of MEPs would be to confirm the appointment of a new team of Commissioners to replace the old lot. As UK Conservatives, we had made it very clear that none of the former members of the discredited Commission should be re-appointed. We had put this into our manifesto very deliberately. The two British Commissioners, Neil Kinnock and Sir Leon Brittan were both technically eligible for re-election. Their hands may have been personally clean, but they were part of a Commission college which had accepted their responsibility was collective and resigned (well, officially anyway). They shouldn't be allowed to un-resign, in our view.

Prime Minister Blair clearly had a very different view. He not only proposed Neil Kinnock again, but even pushed for his selection as a senior Vice-President – in charge of reform. His Labour MEPs immediately voted to approve the new Commission in full, including the re-appointment of four of the discredited previous Commission.

One year after the Wise Men's report and there was little evidence of real change. In April 2000 we refused to sign off the 1998 accounts, as there were still too many loose ends. More significantly, we refused to pass the budget for the year ahead. This time it was Romano Prodi as Commission President who was in the firing line. Many of us felt he should indeed have been fired.

There should be no excuses for the failures of the Commission in managing the various budgets. The lack of basic controls has been appalling. One does not have to be a businessman to realise that. The culture of non-accountability and cover-up has to change. The worry remains that the discipline, and the culture, is still not right.

In May 2002, the EU Commission Chief Accountant Marta Andreasen complained that poor management systems were still leaving the EU budget open to massive fraud. She put the blame firmly on Commissioner Neil Kinnock for talking reform but doing little to deliver it. The good news for us was that she approached UK Conservative MEPs with her story because she knew from our record that we would do something about it. She was of course suspended as a result. Almost immediately there was a leaked paper from the EU Court of Auditors that labelled the Commission's so-called controls as insecure and unreliable. 'Failures abound, and are a waste of public funds. It is impossible to put a figure on the amount involved,' it said. Despite this vindication of her position, she remained suspended. This time it was another Conservative MEP, Chris Heaton-Harris, who took up the cause, rigorously challenging Commissioner Kinnock at every opportunity and highlighting the lack of reforms for which he was officially responsible. As a direct result, Neil Kinnock has had to face a barrage of TV interviews to explain himself and there was even an expectation he might resign.

Meanwhile, the EU Chief Auditor, Jules Muis, volunteered his own resignation in 2003, speaking of his one-man struggle to push the Commission "from the 19th century into the 21st century." He told MEPs of his mounting frustration with an outfit that refused to face its problems, and failed to help him resolve them. When he tried to investigate the latest scandal of funds being siphoned out of EuroStat (the Commission's statistics department), the Commission tied his hands so utterly that he felt he could not do a proper audit. His final, damning verdict on the Commission's lack of interest in reform was: "Eventually the whole thing will implode."

But without diluting the blame on the Commission, there are other morals to be drawn from the above tale of woe, and some clear lessons to be learnt.

The first is that much of the fraud, particularly regarding the agricultural budget, actually takes place in the Member States. It was countries that made the fraudulent claims in the first place. No EU country can escape censure – and the UK is not blameless. The Commission, rightly, gets the flak for not having systems in place to prevent the fraud occurring, to enable it to be detected, and to manage the subsidy programmes efficiently. But national governments, of the left and the right, also bear a heavy responsibility.

Secondly, the problems of lack of control and weak management essentially arise from the quantity of work to be managed and the sheer size of the budget involved. The annual EU budget has risen to around €100 billion and is still rising. This is a massive incentive for fraud. Commissioner Chris Patten recently recalled that in an earlier post as UK Minister for Overseas Development, he had half the level of his current budget but more than twice the people to manage it.

In the EU at the moment there is simply too much money sloshing around to be properly managed without a substantial increase in Commission staff. Rather than have more staff, the solution should be a much smaller budget and many fewer projects. Europe should do less, and do it better.

Thirdly, the European Parliament is substantially at fault too. The Parliament doesn't raise the taxes that will fund the budget. MEPs don't have to provide the money. That makes it all the easier – and all the more irresponsible – for MEPs to vote on how to spend it. Parliament is constantly calling on the Commission to do more work, to become involved in more projects, to increase funding for yet another worthy cause. For the EU to succeed in doing less, MEPs have to stop asking it to do more.

Finally, fraud is fraud is fraud. On such an issue, MEPs should not vote on party political lines. We should vote on principle. Politicians might then get a better reputation for themselves.

That'll be the day.

Chapter Thirteen

Bigger is Beautiful

When I first signed up for this role I didn't know too much about the EU's enlargement plans. I did know that the EU had grown in little spurts from the original six Member States to fifteen. I also knew that each spurt hadn't just made the EU bigger: it also made it more complicated, more diverse and much more remote from the people. In the UK, more people voted to expel Nasty Nick in Big Brother than voted at the 1999 European Parliamentary Elections. The risk is that enlargement to include a further ten countries in 2004 will make it remoter still.

The idea of enlargement on this scale and at this pace was probably never even a distant twinkle in the eyes of the founding fathers. The unforeseen collapse of the Berlin Wall, the ending of the cold war and the lifting of the Iron Curtain bisecting Eastern and Western Europe changed everything. Enlargement to the east is suddenly possible, and the EU has been enthusiastic to embrace a historic opportunity to unite the two halves of divided Europe into a single whole.

Politically it must make good sense to try and bind these ex-communist fledgling democracies into Western European values. We should all want them to feel at home with 'us' lest the curtain comes down again and they find themselves once more on the other side. As ex-Chancellor of Germany Helmut Kohl once said, when challenged as to why he appeared to be making such undue haste to re-integrate Eastern Germany into the fatherland: 'it is important to get the hay into the barn quickly in case it rains'.

The political case for enlargement is strong. Once candidate countries are inside the EU, democratic principles, human rights and the rule of law should become more firmly embedded. Peace on the continent should thereby be made permanent.

Apart from the politics, there is a moral case to be made for enlargement. When the continent was carved up after World War II, many of the candidate countries found themselves the wrong side of the Iron Curtain. It was not their choice. In the decades that followed, such countries saw West Germany, the original aggressor and the cause of their plight, pull away economically as well as politically. They fell further and further behind, condemned to continue as economic laggards through no fault of her own. This injustice needs to be resolved, and their speedy inclusion into the EU would right a great wrong.

A moral case can be made for other countries to become candidates too. It is sometimes forgotten that post-war Europe included a fascist dictatorship in Spain, a Colonels' coup in Greece, and a communist dictatorship in Portugal. Now firmly inside the EU, all three countries have stable democracies, and their earlier lapses are a distant memory. Their absorption of democratic values is substantially due to the stability and moral peer pressure of the rest of the EU – plus the fact that EU laws say that this is the way it has to be.

The hope now is that a similar morality may breed elsewhere. Turkey is keen to climb on board, but is not yet a democracy. The military is in charge, the minority Kurds are unloved, Opposition parties are outlawed if they become inconvenient and human rights are not exactly the accepted norm. For Turkey to join the EU, all this has to change. This should be good for Turkey: it would also be good for the EU.

The European Union should not just be seen as a white Christian club. Muslim countries should be welcome too. As a full member of NATO Turkey should be doubly welcome. Europe should prefer having Turkey within EU boundaries and sharing EU values, rather than excluding it and forcing the country to look for different and more fundamentalist leadership from countries such as Iran.

Another moral case for inclusion in the enlargement process is Cyprus. Whilst the two national Governments in Greece and Turkey now have a more constructive relationship with each other, the two halves of Cyprus have glowered at each other hopelessly for nearly 30 years. The real hope is that entry into the EU as one whole island can put the feuding into perspective and consign it to history. EU democratic values may yet claim another success. There are positive signs at last: the border has been opened between the two halves and Greek Cypriots have not only been allowed to visit their old homes but have been warmly welcomed. The people have been showing the way for the politicians.

Aside from the political and the moral case, the commercial case for general enlargement is also strong. More countries would make the Single Market much bigger, and therefore automatically more beautiful for business, for employers, for workers and for consumers. The 15 current Member States total around 370 million people. After enlargement, this could rise to fully 500 million. Size is strength. Such a market would be bigger than the USA and Japan combined and should give progressively greater prosperity to all within.

However some existing Member States are nervous. Austria is worried about immigration. Already Austria has absorbed some one million immigrants within its population of eight million: she is not eager for more. She fears thousands more of unskilled, cheap workers will flow in: the fear of the candidate countries is that it will be the skilled workers who do the flowing.

France is worried about losing much of its hefty agricultural subsidies under a changed CAP: France eats up around half of the €46 billion subsidy available to all EU Member States each year. France is also very aware that Poland alone has more farmers than the current fifteen Member States put together. The Common Agricultural Policy will have to change radically as a result of enlargement, and France could be the biggest loser long term.

Spain is worried about losing its 'structural funds': at present she qualifies for a special subsidy because the economies of so many Spanish regions are below 75% of the Community average. Of all the funds available within the current EU, Spain is at present entitled to a massive 62%. After enlargement, and the inclusion of so many very poor countries, the EU average will be automatically lower. Most Spanish regions will suddenly be above 75% of the new lower average. Spanish subsidies will substantially disappear. Poorer Eastern and Central European Countries will get the subsidies instead and rightly so – but this is not an argument easily sold in Spain.

Germany welcomes enlargement in principle (well, for the former communist countries anyway) but is worried about the cost. Germany is currently the largest net contributor to the EU budget and is not enthusiastic about the prospect of an even bigger bill – especially as she is still paying a hefty price for the rebuilding of the former East Germany. Berlin alone is already twenty billion dollars in debt, and more bills are still coming in.

Of course the prospect of enlargement promoting European peace is to some people simplistic. The European Union will still have a boundary. However many countries are inside that boundary, a boundary there still will be. However many countries are included, by definition there must always be some countries outside.

Russia is likely to be one of those remaining outside. Its history, its values and its size all tend to preclude it. In the beginning the EU boundaries were far away from Russia. The old USSR had many tame satellites as a buffer in between. As those satellites fold into the EU, as the EU boundary comes ever closer, this will scarcely make the Russians feel less threatened.

Kaliningrad is a special problem. Formerly Konigsberg and part of Germany, it has since World War Two been a Russian enclave, isolated from the rest of the country. As a key port, and as home to the Soviet submarine fleet, it is not about to join the West even if that option were available. It is physically decaying, is environmentally appalling, is morally corrupt, and is bristling with nuclear weapons. Its main exports are crime, drugs, prostitution and pollution.

But it is Russian. And instead of being enclosed by fellow communist countries, within which her population had complete freedom of movement, she may soon be marooned. Those countries may soon become EU Member States, with their own border controls. To make matters worse, neighbouring Lithuania has applied to join NATO.

Meanwhile, what of the candidate countries themselves? What might membership do for them?

The simple answer is that the ex-Eastern bloc countries believe their ramshackle economies will be transformed by membership of the world's largest trading bloc, and the small islands of Malta and Cyprus don't want to be left isolated. Collectively they have a long way to go to catch up. Combined, they will add about a third to the EU's land area, and around 20% to its population – but less than ten per cent to the EU economy. They are looking for money to grow their economies. They need lots of it.

They are not going to get it. There is simply not enough money in the pot, and Member States are unwilling to make the pot bigger. As a result, the funds available to farmers under the CAP will be less than half that available to the existing Fifteen. Even this will be phased in gradually over ten years. It is no surprise that some in the candidate countries have complained that they are being offered second-class citizenship.

Despite that, the referendum vote in each of the candidate countries has been overwhelmingly in favour. The people are not just looking for a quick economic fix: they are looking to be finally re-united with the west. Soon after the vote in Hungary I was speaking to a Hungarian businesswoman. She told me that when the result was announced she cried and cried for joy. She had tears in her eyes again as she relived the moment. For her, EU membership meant that the division of Europe was finally over and could never return. Such an emotional attachment to the EU may seem strange to us, but to her and others like her it is central. As an aside I was reminded how business is already ahead of the politicians in bringing Europe closer together: she was a local Director of Tesco.

Some countries will have longer to wait before they join. Croatia and Romania are amongst those in the process of applying. But to succeed, every candidate has to sign up to all existing EU legislation, the 80,000 pages of the Acquis Communautaire – conveniently parcelled up into 31 oh-so-easy-to-read chapters. By mid-2001 Romania had only managed to sign off agreement on 6 – and hadn't even got around to translating the last 16 into their own language.

Romania certainly has a major challenge, even to be considered as part of a second wave of applicants from 2006 onwards. That is why I thought it a good place to visit beforehand.

The Employment and Social Affairs Committee had the chance to send a small delegation of four MEPs to assess the country's progress on transposing EU social legislation into their own national law. I had been to Romania many years before during the Ceausescu era in the early eighties, staying with our friends the Markhams. Derek was Mr Shell out there, later to reappear alongside me canvassing in Burton-on-Trent at the European Parliamentary elections.

The country then was clearly in its own closed world. It would be fascinating to see to what extent it had changed.

When I landed late on the Sunday evening, the visible difference was immediate. To begin with, getting through passport control took a mere five minutes, as opposed to the half-hour of close questioning and baggage searching of the previous visit. I was able to get a taxi without being closely scrutinised by police. And as we drove away I noticed the bright lights along the motorway – an unaffordable extravagance in the past unless Ceausescu just happened to be using the road.

The taxi-driver gave me an early insight into the new Romania, in particular as far as the relevance of rule of law was concerned. When I got into the cab I instinctively buckled my seat belt, to be immediately told by the driver that there was no need in Bucharest because density of the traffic jams meant that there was no danger. He then blasted off at high speed, never stopping once until we reached our hotel.

Bucharest had certainly changed. Not only were there now plush international hotels, but the people on the streets were brightly dressed and talking into their mobile phones. There were plenty of items to buy in the shops: last time around they were mainly closed, officially for 'stocktaking', but in reality because in those days they had no stock to sell.

Last time, the effective local currency consisted of packets of Kent cigarettes. Flashing foreign currency was illegal, but foreign cigarettes were fine. This time US dollars were remarkably welcome, and advertising hoardings proudly proclaimed '<u>New</u> Kent' cigarettes. Romania was clearly learning fast.

We were invited to visit a paint factory, to see how EU health and safety regulations were being fully implemented. The factory was specially chosen for the purpose. The presentation from the management was good, and the visit was going well – until we actually visited the shop floor. The technology was quite new for Romania, a mere twenty years old. The machines had all been freshly painted in our honour. The paint fumes were extremely unpleasant, and there was no proper air filtration. The workers had all been issued with suspiciously new-looking facemasks, but these had all been pushed to the top of their heads. It was too hot to wear the masks, and like the seat belts in the taxi they were merely there for show.

Outside, there were pits filled with foetid water, which I inspected when nobody was looking. When I later asked, from a distance, what was in these pits I was told with a straight face that it was waste water that was regularly recycled. The scum on top confirmed that the water hadn't moved in weeks.

If this was the model factory, we wondered what the others must be like.

I rather wished we could have gone just north of Bucharest to the town of Cormarnec, on the road to Ploesti. Back in 1980 I recalled that the local cement factory used to spew out so much of its product into the atmosphere that all the buildings and all the trees were permanently grey-white. I suspected that the lungs of the locals had a similar tinge. I also suspected that not much had changed in the past 20 years.

There wasn't time to go out to check, but the paint-factory experience compelled me to ask the Commission organiser whether we might have time to visit the city's waste water treatment plant. This was promptly set up without difficulty for 8am the following morning, which meant another early start. It was worth it.

The plant was constructed on a giant scale, typical of Ceausescu. A wide canal had been dug to take the cleaned water to the river beyond. There was a special widened part for all the pleasure boats that would of course wish to tie up there.

There were no boats. There was no cleaned water. The plant had never worked. Ceausescu had insisted that all the parts were made in Romania partly for national pride and partly because there was no foreign currency to buy the real thing. But they couldn't make the parts to the right quality, so the whole plant lay idle. In rainy weather as much as 100 cubic metres of water a second streamed into the plant for treatment. It streamed straight out of the other end, untreated, directly into the Danube.

The country has an immense need to update its transport system. It needs some €11 billion to sort it out, and its transport budget is pitifully small. Meanwhile its waste water treatment needs fully €22 billion, and yet has only one twentieth of the annual transport budget. With inflation running at over 2% a month, and an average income of only €100 a head, the country just doesn't have the money.

There is no way that Romania can comfortably meet EU environmental standards, but the country has not asked for any extended transition period before she has to conform. Officially, the reason is that Romanian standards are tighter than EU standards, so no derogations are necessary. Unofficially, given that she is nowhere near meeting any standards, it doesn't matter what she signs up to. For the same reason, Romania has proudly proclaimed that she was one of the first countries to sign the Kyoto Protocol on climate change. I did not find this reassuring.

There is an old saying: 'When in Rome, do as the Romans do'. Maybe there should be a new version: 'When in Romania, say what people want to hear but do nothing.'

The people we spoke to were clear about the implications of joining the EU. The upside was very clear: joining would bring Freedom, both economic and political. But they also saw a downside: the biggest problem could be disillusion when their lives were not instantaneously transformed. Their own few internal reforms had so far brought only more poverty. It was no surprise that many people still put fresh flowers on Ceausescu's grave.

None of the above is presented as an argument for keeping out Romania, or indeed any other candidate country. But it is an argument for being realistic about what candidates can and can't do.

And this is where the argument gets really interesting. The OECD has published a deep analysis of the economic problems facing Romania, given its clapped-out factories and reliance on unwieldy state manufacturing monopolies. It observes that massive restructuring is required, and that considerable job losses will be needed over a short period. In passing, it observes that EU employment protection legislation is far from a solution to Romania's problem – such laws actually compound the problem by making restructuring more difficult. Romania may be an extreme example of this, which is why it is not joining in 2004, but it is still an example of difficulties experienced to a varying extent by most candidate countries.

The lesson is clear: one-size-fits-all EU legislation does not fit all at all. It is not the candidates that should change, it is the concept of how much legislation is actually appropriate at EU level in the first place.

John Major was one of the leading promoters of enlargement when he was Prime Minister, and not just for the reasons given at the start of this chapter. A further reason, beloved of any Conservative Prime Minister, was that ex-communist countries have become largely conservative. They have seen the follies and the failures of Socialism and collectivism at first hand: they would not willingly repeat the experience. This was confirmed to me at an Employment Conference in Austria. The Slovak delegate said that in the past his country had been ruled successively by Vienna, by Berlin, and by Moscow. There was no wish now to be ruled by Brussels.

It has been forty years since the original six Member States came together to form what was then called the European Economic Community. Since then membership has more than doubled. The name has changed twice, but the basic structures and institutions have barely altered. They have been stretched almost to breaking point but they are still essentially the same. Enlargement will force massive change on the way the EU does business, and indeed on what business it should do. All the jigsaw pieces will be thrown up in the air: the question is, what picture will they make when they land?

One vision of such a future Europe is that more will need to be decided at the centre. This is very much the Socialist, corporatist view. To manage a sprawling empire, a strong emperor is required. This is the concept of the so-called deeper Europe, so favoured by the federalists.

The alternative vision of a wider, shallower Europe holds the brighter future. With membership of at least 25 countries, the EU cannot expect to operate with all key decisions taken unanimously. But neither can it operate with too many decisions taken by qualified majority vote, with the bigger countries' wishes being blocked by a coalition of smaller ones, or vice versa. There will need to be a general consensus on broad directions. But detailed one-size-fits-all policies, going into finest prescriptive detail on what must be done at every national level: this approach should have to be binned.

Several years ago, the former Czech Prime Minister, Vaclav Klaus, commented on the EU. He said: 'the prevailing system is too heavy because of over regulation; too socialist because of generous welfare state transfer payments…too closed because of the high degree of protectionism; too slow because of bureaucratic and administrative procedures; and too costly because of all of these things'. It was a perceptive analysis of the past and the present: it must not continue to be true into the future.

Enlargement will drive massive change in the role and the operation of the European Union. Such change should be embraced with enthusiasm. The EU should be compelled to do much less, and to do it a darn sight better.

This is the third reason for enlargement, and one of the best reasons of all.

If such change happens, when such change happens, bigger will be much more beautiful indeed.

Chapter Fourteen

Not Nice Treaties

Governments do like signing Treaties. They feel it is a very governmental thing to do.

EU Member State Governments have extra reasons for liking them. If they can secure a Treaty during their six-month rotating Presidency of the EU, they can brand such a Treaty with the name of the city where the treaty was signed. This ensures their particular Presidency is immortalised.

Cynics might suggest that this is why Europe churns out so many Treaties.

The development of the EU has certainly been marked by a tirade of Treaties over the years. Each Treaty moved the Member States further along the road of 'ever closer union' foreseen in the original founding Treaty of Rome. Early Treaties are no longer well remembered: it is the recent ones that loom largest in the public minds – and in the public fears.

The one that still raises a shudder amongst hardened Euro-sceptics is the Treaty of Maastricht.

The original draft of this Treaty was actually put together by Luxembourg. The outline was handed over when the Netherlands assumed the Presidency in July 1991. The Dutch immediately scrapped the draft and started again: they wanted it to be all their very own work. John Major in his autobiography describes the general reaction:

'Their document was catastrophic. They seemed to have swept up the nightmares of every anti-European propagandist and put them into their text: new powers to decide foreign policy and home affairs at Community level; more authority for the European Court of Justice; power for the European Parliament to overrule decisions taken by sovereign governments; more majority voting to decide issues of social affairs, health and education. In short: a United States of Europe.'

The first key issue was the Single Currency. European Monetary Union had been hinted at in the original Treaty of Rome, but had remained just an aspiration. The Treaty of Maastricht now laid it out as a commitment. It would no longer be a possible step in the future: it was a definite step and it was now.

The second issue was the formal inclusion of a Social Chapter. Continental Europe had been very proud of the development of the 'European Social Model'. Essentially this guaranteed a high level of worker protection, both in and out of work. Socialists loved it. Employers were less impressed, as legislation ensured high costs with low flexibility and essentially encouraged them to avoid hiring employees in the first place. Putting this formally into a Treaty with its own special Chapter simply signalled open season for more such laws.

The UK Government was proud of the country's employment record, and proud too that its climate of industrial relations was so positive. We didn't need more red tape on our employers. We didn't see why the EU should meddle in our business: Social Affairs were a Member State competence and the UK felt should remain so.

On both these critical issues John Major managed to get his way. Firstly he managed to negotiate an opt-out on the Single Currency: other countries could commit to sign up immediately, but the UK had the right to stay out forever if it wished. He also managed to wrench an opt-out for the UK from the Social Chapter.

He even succeeded in writing into the Treaty a key clause on subsidiarity. This secured unanimous acceptance for the very first time that decisions would only be taken at EU level when they concerned bigger issues than individual Member States could sensibly handle on their own. Otherwise decisions would be taken at the national, or indeed regional level as appropriate. This really seemed to be one in the eye for the onward march of federalism. The UK Press agreed it was game, set and match to the UK, and hailed John Major as a hero.

His opponents thought otherwise – and his main opponents were in the Conservative Party.

Earlier Treaties had advanced the cause of a federal EU, but Margaret Thatcher had signed those which apparently made them alright. The Maastricht Treaty was the one seen as a Treaty too far. A united stand had to be made against a United States of Europe. The Maastricht rebels as they were to be known, a group which included the future Conservative Party leader Iain Duncan Smith, were determined to make this stand on principle.

For them, a visible proof of the emerging superstate was the agreement in the Treaty that every citizen of any EU Member State was automatically a citizen of the EU, with rights to move freely, work and vote in another Member State. National passports would be scrapped, in exchange for a standardised EU document. There would be a token royal coat of arms on the UK version, but the Superstate was giving its own passport to its own citizens.

There were other signs too, such as a move towards a common EU Foreign & Security Policy – which might have meant the UK asking EU permission to take back the Falklands.

There would be more use of Qualified Majority Voting (QMV), which meant the UK surrendering its veto in yet more areas. In practice it also meant other countries surrendering their veto in these same areas, to pull down a few more protectionist barriers holding up the completion of the Single Market. But it confirmed the concerns of those who feared the final demise of the nation state.

The UK Parliament ratified the Treaty in the end, taking the view that the opt-outs meant the Treaty was just about liveable with. But the Government was fatally weakened in the process as deep internal divisions were laid bare for all to see.

Meanwhile President Chirac of France wanted his own trophy treaty. With enlargement coming up, and new voting procedures across a larger membership needing to be established rapidly, the opportunity was there. At the end of the French Presidency he finally got his Treaty, signed after five laborious days in Nice.

Promoted as a triumph of French diplomacy, Chirac hailed the session as "one of the great European summits." Others called it the clumsiest of compromises, and it was widely derided even as it was being signed. It was certainly a remarkable achievement: never in the field of European Treaties had so many Governments been made so unhappy at the same time.

Essentially the Treaty tried to resolve the numbers game after enlargement, namely how many:
1) Commissioners there should be;
2) Votes per country there should be;
3) MEPs there should be.

Agreement was indeed cobbled together on all three questions, but the answer in each case was a mess.

In the 1999-2004 Commission there were 20 Commissioners for the fifteen Member States, with the larger countries having two each. Officially it ought to make no difference to a Member State how many Commissioners it has. Commissioners don't have national portfolios: their mission is not to represent their home country but to lie back and think of Europe.

In practice Member States still regard the idea of having their 'own' Commissioner as a matter of national prestige. So it was agreed that as from 2005 the big countries would reduce to one Commissioner each and that the total number would rise on the basis of one Commissioner per country to an absolute maximum of 27. What happens when there would be more than 27 countries would have been anyone's guess. My guess is that there would simply be another Treaty.

Meanwhile, the idea of one Commissioner per country looks like a straightforward solution. It isn't. It would result in more bureaucracy for no benefit. New portfolios would have to be created to find work for them to do. Each would have to have staff. And a budget. It would be very much a move in the wrong direction.

The second question, deciding on the re-weighting of votes per country in the Council of Ministers, was bound to be difficult. Ostensibly about revising the decision process, the argument was really all about how to let the new Members share power without the existing Member States losing any of their own. The result was another mess.

The original 15 countries had 87 votes between them in the Council of Ministers: as negotiations continued the total number of votes for an enlarged EU membership needed to grow to 342 for the mathematical subdivision to work out.

The total votes available thus grew nearly fourfold. The largest countries, Germany, France, Italy and UK went up nearly threefold from 10 to 29 votes. Spain more than trebled from 8 to 27. Smaller countries with less clout did less well, with most existing small Member States only growing between two and two and a half times.

But this cumbersome re-weighting of votes was just the first step. In the good old days of 15 Member States, a decision under QMV would prevail if 62 votes were cast in favour out of the total of 87. This was clearly far too simple. After enlargement, decisions would only pass if there was a 'triple majority', which was Euro-jargon for the following:-

a) A specified number of votes must be in favour;
b) A majority of the number of Member States must also be in favour;
c) Countries representing at least 62% of the total EU population must be in favour too.

Some statisticians later concluded that there would be only a 2.6% chance of any majority decision ever being reached at all in future.

The total number of MEPs from the existing fifteen Member States was 626. An earlier Treaty had capped it for all time at a maximum of 700 after full enlargement. But however many ways Chirac tried to cut 700, he could never secure agreement on the slices. So the numbers edged up and up until Nice finally established a new maximum of 732.

197 of the larger total of MEPs would come from the current candidate countries – which meant a reduced number from existing Member States.

In common with France and Italy, the UK will reduce progressively from 87 MEPs to 72 as more countries join. However it was agreed that Germany currently on 99 MEPs would stay at 99 even after enlargement, the only country to keep its tally intact. This was in exchange for not increasing the votes for Germany in the Council, despite her increase in size following the absorption of the former East Germany.

This concession by other Member States was enormous. The enhanced dominance of German MEPs will strengthen their relative voting power significantly, enabling them to vote themselves even more easily into key positions of influence within the Parliament.

However, none of the above issues gave grandeur or glamour to the Treaty. Treaties do try to be both glamorous and grand. So the French Presidency inserted other issues into the final document. The grandest was the European Security and Defence Policy, also known as the Rapid Reaction Force, a.k.a. the European Army.

The official idea was spun as follows: if NATO didn't want to get involved in a problem in Europe's own backyard, such as next time round in the

Balkans, then Europe should be in a position to take appropriate action to sort things out on its own. This meant that the EU had to be in a position to deploy troops without relying on NATO at all.

Some of us were – and are – extremely worried about this. Central to the security of Europe for the past fifty years has been NATO. Central to NATO has been the involvement of the USA.

Sadly not every country thinks the same. The French have never been happy with NATO precisely because of American involvement. France withdrew from Nato's integrated military structure back in 1967. France regards America's strength in Europe as a challenge to the importance of France. One of her ongoing foreign policy objectives, in the words of President Chirac himself, has been 'to contain' America. This is why she came up with the idea of an alternative, European led, defence force specifically in order to sideline the United States. It is also another reason France opposed George Bush over Iraq.

Jean-Pierre Kelche, Chief of the French Defence Staff confirmed to the *Daily Telegraph* in March 2001 that 'the EU must be able to act alone. Europe is an enormous economic power, but not yet a mature military power'. The French have made no secret of their ambition to see this change.

The Nice Treaty was agreed in December 2000. The Irish decided to hold a Referendum six months later and the result was a decisive 'No'. The EU response was to prod them to have a second referendum a year later. This time, the vote was 'Yes' – but only just. Any future Treaty may not be so lucky.

If previous Treaties were thought to be significant, the next one looming on the horizon will be critical. The plan is for a new Treaty of Rome in 2004, to replace the earlier Treaties and pull together the work of a special European Convention under French ex-President Giscard d'Estaing.

Recognising that fewer and fewer people voted in successive European

Parliamentary elections, the original concept of the Convention was to make the EU more transparent, more democratic and more efficient – in short, to bring the EU 'closer to its citizens'. In practice, the Convention has produced a new Constitution for Europe, which risks making it even more remote.

There is a proposal for a single powerful President of the European Council, which will please Tony Blair as he clearly wants the job. There will be an EU Foreign Minister to handle a Common EU Foreign & Security Policy. There is even a proposal for a single Finance Minister to 'ensure co-ordination' of economic and employment policy across all Member States.

(Do we want our policies to be co-ordinated with the sagging economic performance of Germany? How will that be good for UK businesses, or indeed for jobs anywhere in Europe for that matter?)

For the first time, the EU would have the power to 'ensure security of energy supplies in the EU'. (Would that mean the UK would lose control of our own oil and gas reserves in the same way we have lost control of 'our' fish in our own territorial waters?)

The EU would become a 'legal personality', able to sign agreements and have a seat in international organisations: this could include replacing EU Member States on the UN Security Council.

There would be a move towards EU harmonisation of criminal law in areas such as the rights of individuals in criminal procedures and the rights of victims of crime; for the first time, the European Parliament would gain the right to legislate on justice and home affairs. There is an intention to give legal force to the so-called Charter of Fundamental Rights, which will be good business for lawyers but bad for everybody else. Finally the national veto would disappear in at least 20 separate policy areas, including asylum policy.

Some want the proposals to go even further, the UK Liberal Democrats for a start. Their representative on the Convention has urged the EU to decide some of our taxes for us.

Altogether there are some 59 separate Treaty Articles. While the detail will be subject to further negotiation by Member State Governments between now and Spring 2004, the general outline is already clear. Despite including some sensible suggestions that dispose of the dottier decisions of Nice, many believe the overall proposals look remarkably like a plan for a Federal Government of Europe. Meanwhile Tony Blair maintains that the draft is a good basis for a final text and takes into account most of the UK concerns. Who do the British people think is right?

There is an easy way to find out. Ask them.

France, Spain, Ireland and Denmark have already declared they will hold a referendum. Other Member States are expected to follow suit. Such countries recognise the proposed Treaty changes are not simply a tidying-up exercise, as fatuously claimed by the UK Government. They see them as having huge constitutional significance. That is why Iain Duncan Smith is so right to call for a referendum for the UK, knowing that he does not just speak for the Conservatives but also speaks for the country.

Tony Blair is refusing a referendum for one very simple reason: it is always dangerous to ask the people.

Like the Irish first time around, they might give the right answer.

Chapter Fifteen

EMU – the bird that just can't fly

There will however definitely be a referendum during this Parliament on the Single Currency. Or not. Tony and Gordon are absolutely united on this: if only they were.

For many people in the UK – certainly many businesses – the biggest single issue of the decade is whether to sign up to the Euro and join the European Monetary Union (EMU). They are looking to the Government for leadership and they are not getting it.

For some a single currency is simply a great idea.

If we all shared the same currency, then we wouldn't have to change in and out of sterling every time we went on holiday, with the banks taking a commission both ways. Exporting/importing companies would no longer get their fingers burnt when different currencies fluctuated against each other. Prices in different EU countries could be more easily compared, which might incidentally stimulate competition and bring prices down. After all, we are supposed to be in the same Single Market.

These are powerful arguments, clearly accepted by twelve EU Governments. Anyway the Euro now exists for 300 million Europeans. Maybe the UK should join? What could be the catch?

The catch of the Single Currency is that it is Single, a One-Size-Fits-All confection that tries to straddle a variety of different economic circumstances. It is only likely to work under certain specific and limited conditions. It can work with small, adjacent countries such as Belgium and Luxembourg, whose economies are interdependent and therefore match each other closely: their currencies have in practice been interchangeable for many years. It can work within a giant country such as the USA, despite a wide variation in economic strength between the various states: it works there because there is political union with a single overall government and a single overall taxation policy.

But throughout history there has never been an example of a successful monetary union of strong but separate and independent countries that have kept their individual economies under their own national control. It has been tried over the centuries and it has failed every time.

The most recent failure was in 1992 when the UK was part of the Exchange Rate Mechanism (ERM). This was the predecessor of the Euro: leading European currencies kept their own separate national identities but broadly locked together at an agreed exchange rate. The three major UK political parties all supported the principle, as did the CBI and the TUC. It seemed a good idea at the time.

It clearly became a very bad idea soon afterwards. Unlike our EU partners, the UK economy went into recession. The currency couldn't flex and take the strain because it was fixed. Jobs took the strain instead. Unemployment shot up as UK companies went bust. In 1989, the year before we joined, some 22,000 businesses failed. By 1992 failures leapt to around 63,000, nearly treble the level a mere three years earlier. Unemployment doubled, and as the economy went deeper into recession the new phrase 'negative equity' emerged. Well over a million households had mortgages that were higher than the value of their property. The interest rate was completely wrong for the UK economy, but as members of the ERM we were stuck with it.

We had to exit the ERM – and the good news was that at least under that system we were able to come out. The pound immediately dropped once the currency was freed from its straitjacket. Interest rates fell to 6% within a few months, and jobs and the economy took off. The UK is still reaping the benefits of the freedom to manage our own economy, though naturally it is the Labour Government that is getting the credit and of course claiming it. That's called politics.

177

The reason why some currencies fluctuate against each other is because they need to. Different national economies tend to move in different cycles, strengthening or weakening, and their currencies need to reflect what is going on.

'Euroland', that is to say the 12 member states currently signed up to the Euro, exports only 10% of its output beyond its borders. Because 90% of trade is with other members, their economies are much more likely to move in step with each other. In reality, they also have had problems with the Euro.

Sir Eddie George, Governor of the Bank of England, said a year before the Euro's formal launch how difficult it was to set the right interest rate for sterling to cope with a booming UK services sector and sluggish manufacturing. If it is hard to set a single interest rate to suit the varying needs within one country, how much harder must it be for a single interest rate to suit the differing needs of 12 different countries?

With a single currency there has to be a single interest rate amongst all participating countries. If any one country offered a higher rate all the funds would flock to that one country. So it has to be the same everywhere – and therein lies the problem.

Ireland's economy has taken off, but their high growth has brought high and growing inflation. At one stage it rose to a 15-year high of 5.2%, three times the EU average. The housing market surged: low real interest rates fuelled high spending. Ireland needed a much higher interest rate to slow the economy down, and curb the price of imports. It couldn't get it.

As its total economy is only around 1% of the whole of Euroland, its voice is too small to be heard. That didn't stop the ECB lecturing Ireland, telling the Irish exactly what they should do. The Irish Government immediately told the Central Bank what it should do.

At the other end of the scale Germany, the largest Euroland economy, is not amused either. It used to have the strongest currency in Europe.

Now some Germans refer locally to the Euro as the 'EU-zloty', a reference to the currency of their weaker Polish neighbour. Others have termed it a "camembert currency" because it is soft, made in France, and smells!

The German people had no say in the decision to join the Single Currency. The politicians decided, and the people are far from happy. Germany is still paying for the high costs of reunification with the East. It has low growth, and unemployment approaching five million. It desperately needs a reduction in interest rates to get its economy back on track, together with a liberalisation of its rigid labour laws. The current ECB policy has done Germany's growth prospects no good at all.

Southern Mediterranean countries have had other worries. Their productivity is miles behind Germany. This means that these countries are likely to suffer much higher inflation. But they cannot vary their national interest rates to help tackle their national problem.

The point is that each country may require a different interest rate to suit its different economic circumstances. Under the Single Currency, they have to have the same one. And there is nothing any of them can do about it. Even Wim Duisenberg has found this out himself. His original brief was to ensure that Euroland interest rates were set so as to ensure overall Euroland inflation is within a 0% and 2% band. During the first 36 months of EU currencies locking together, inflation was outside this band more than half the time. The problem is that a one-size-fits-all interest rate doesn't fit anybody.

Locking our own currency to that of our continental partners would create especial problems for the UK. Our economy is so very different from the rest of the EU. We are the only 'petro-currency', i.e. a net exporter of oil and gas. We have more home-owners, therefore more personal savings tied up in property, often on variable mortgages as opposed to the long-term fixed mortgages in Euroland: changes in short-term interest rates therefore have a more destabilising effect on the UK economy. We have a much more significant financial services industry: more people work in the City of London than actually live in the whole of Frankfurt, home of the European Central Bank (ECB). We also do a much higher proportion of our trade in US dollars than any other EU Member State.

The UK sends around half its exports to Euroland and less than 20% of its total output. We have much more global trade which leaves our economy more exposed to other currency fluctuations.

So there has to be a major question as to whether the UK should try to force-fit itself into the Single Currency irrespective of whether or not it works in Euroland.

Gordon Brown wanted to keep control of the question, or at least the answer, by inventing five tests. Will the Euro promote higher growth and a lasting increase in jobs? Has our business cycle converged with Euroland, and if so will it stay converged? Is our economy flexible enough to adapt to changes? Will the impact on long-term investment into the UK be positive? Would the Euro put at risk the competitive position of our financial services sector?

After two years' exhaustive study, only the last test has apparently been passed. The other four have failed. With only a 20% pass rate, the answer should logically be No we should not join. The Chancellor's answer seems to be that we should keep taking the tests every year until they are all passed. This is a recipe for dither and uncertainty, the last thing business needs.

Meanwhile the plan is that as Europe enlarges each candidate country will also sign up to the Euro. The same single interest rate will then have to span these young and fragile economies as well. By 2006 the Single Currency should include the Hungarian Forint, the Czech Koruna, the Slovenian Tolar, the Lithuanian Litas and the Latvian Lat. Such a move will not exactly stabilise the Euro, as the one average interest rate will try to grapple with a wider and wider range of differing economic needs.

So if the Euro in practice is so suspect, why are so many different people and different countries pushing for it?

France wanted a single currency because it was fed up with having the German Mark as the master currency on the continent. It wanted its exchange rate fixed while the Deutschmark was strong in order to lock in a competitive advantage for France. Germany signed up as the price of agreement to go ahead with reunification. Otherwise France would have vetoed it. Smaller countries wanted a single currency to protect their own smaller currencies from being buffeted by speculators. They would also be able to borrow more cheaply because lenders would have more confidence in the larger currency. The candidate countries from Eastern Europe want it in order to lock into the success of the capitalist west.

Tony Blair wants it because he believes that somehow this will put us more 'at the heart of Europe', and we will be able to influence more decisions in a way favourable to the UK. Some leading Tory ex-heavyweights want it because they feel that to be anti-Euro means to be anti-European. They also believe that the Single Currency will compel Member States to tackle their rigid labour markets and high cost/high regulation cultures, even though experience to-date suggests the exact opposite.

Some multi-nationals want it as it would put their costs on a stable playing field relative to other Euroland trading partners or competitors. It saves them money, and they are not too fussed if unemployment grows in one area and declines in another: they can easily shift production around between different European countries.

Many continental consumers want it because they have become fed up with handling different currencies. Border zones between some countries are densely populated, and many border towns have struggled with several different national currencies for years as workers and shoppers move between countries every day.

Politicians want it because the original purpose of the Single Currency was not economic but political. The Prime Minister dares not admit that this is the agenda. Others have been more open and more honest.

Former German Chancellor Helmut Kohl has said: "We want the political unification of Europe. Without monetary union there cannot be political union and vice versa."

Romano Prodi, President of the European Commission, has gone on the record: "The Euro can only lead to closer and closer integration of countries' economic policies. This demands that Member States give up more sovereignty."

Wim Duisenberg, President of the European Central Bank, concluded: "The process of monetary union goes hand in hand, must go hand in hand, with political integration and ultimately political union. EMU is, and was always meant to be, a stepping stone to a United Europe."

The Euro is not just a Single Currency. EMU stands for European Monetary Union. It is only through such complete union that the Euro will succeed.

For a single interest rate to become right for everybody means there has to be a single economy. EMU effectively means there would no longer be separate national economies, independently run. It would mean one giant single economy run centrally, whether from Brussels or from Frankfurt.

A single economy ultimately means there has to be common taxation across Euroland. In the case of the UK, our taxes would have to go up sharply. A single economy means common treatment of pensions. I am often getting letters from UK pensioners asking why UK pensions cannot be as high as they appear to be in the EU. The reason is that other EU countries have made pension promises which they cannot keep. The current generation of workers is officially paying, through taxation, for the pensions of the previous generation. But as pensioners live longer, the money in Euroland is no longer sufficient to cover the commitments. The International Monetary Fund (IMF) reported a few years ago that unfunded pension liabilities in the UK were just 10% of GDP. Italy was 75%, Germany 110% and France 115%. Taxation and/or borrowing in Euroland will need to go up hugely to fund the difference. Interest rates would have to move in consequence, and the value of the currency would also be sharply affected. If we were signed up, our economy would suffer for the common EU good.

Commissioner Frits Bolkestein says a good time to judge the success of the Single Currency would be 2010. Then those people born in the 'baby-boom' of 1945 would be 65. There would be surge in pension demand. The shortfall would suddenly be obvious. The problem would have to be tackled.

No wonder the rest of Euroland want us in. The UK could help fund the shortfall. They also want us in, of course, because as a sound and strong economy the UK would be seen to buttress the strength of the Euro. They are also well aware that our subscribing to the same high level of social costs and taxation as themselves would blunt our competitive advantage over them. They would not find this a problem.

Essentially and irrevocably, if we were to sign up to EMU we would no longer be able to determine the economic governance of our own country. It is significant that the European Convention has proposed a single Finance Minister for Euroland. For many, this issue of sovereignty is not just the biggest issue: it is the only issue.

Our democratic tradition lets the people decide who should be in charge. If we don't like what they do, we can 'throw the rascals out'. If the rascals have little influence over what goes on, then there's little point in throwing them out – or even throwing them in in the first place. Under EMU, those guiding the economy would no longer be responsible to the British electorate – or indeed directly responsible to any electorate. That is not why we joined the EU.

Some say there is no such danger, that our sovereignty will not be diminished and that the Euro can be a successful currency without leading to a central superstate. If this is true, time will tell: let us see what happens in Euroland over a full economic cycle, what happens when yet more countries join, and also how much flexing against the Euro the £ will have needed during this same period.

Some say that aligning our very different economy to the Euro is unlikely to create the problems of the ERM. Why not? This is a gigantic experiment, with no exit if it proves wrong. No sensible businessman would take such a one-way risk with his company. Dare we take such a risk with our country?

Some say that the Euro is inevitable for the UK because it now exists on the continent. This is simply Labour spin.

Others say we have no choice, that the UK cannot possibly prosper outside the Single Currency. Certainly it is not easy having a currency which varies against a major trading partner. But we are currently prospering rather well.

London continues to dominate the world of financial services, including insurance and cross-border bank lending. The UK share of global foreign exchange business is over 30%. The rest of Europe put together has only 23%. Even the USA only has 18%.

London is ranked number one in the world for the management of institutional equities, five times more than Paris and fully nine times more than Frankfurt. Funds managed in the UK for overseas clients have grown fourfold since 1992. The UK also remains the largest market for inward investment within the EU.

Sir Eddie George has admitted that the City has prospered since the launch of the Euro. "There were those who argued that the City would suffer if the UK failed to join from the outset. That clearly has not so far happened – quite the reverse." He later added that a fluctuating exchange rate can enable a stable economy; that conversely a fixed exchange rate can make an economy unstable. With such heretical remarks, his knighthood must have been touch and go.

The UK is now the world's fourth or fifth largest economy. Growth in recent years has been ahead of our EU partners. Our job creation record has been much better too, because of our more flexible labour markets following trade union reform and the much more business-friendly regulation of the 1980's and early 1990's. It is twisting the facts for Euro-supporters to claim that UK jobs will somehow be lost if we don't sign up rapidly: Euroland unemployment is much higher than the UK, and is still rising.

Some say that you cannot be 'half-in and half-out' of Europe, as if that was an accurate reflection of a policy of being within the EU but outside the Euro. Yet the UK is one of the few EU members to be outside the Schengen zone (the passport-free continent) because we require to control immigration. That has been accepted without any difficulty by the other Member States. There has been no suggestion that we have to sign up in order to fully belong to the EU. Similarly, we achieved an opt-out from joining the Single Currency. This was approved unanimously by the European Council. Other Member States would never have readily agreed to this if it had meant being half-out of Europe. We can be in Europe, but not run by Europe. We do have a choice.

The Danes had that choice back in 2000. Their vote against joining the Single Currency was decisive. It was also remarkable.

All the media, all five political parties in Denmark, and almost all business and trade unions were united in supporting a Yes vote. Remarkably, the people decided for themselves. They voted a resounding No. Remarkably too, nearly 90% of the people voted.

For the people of Denmark, joining the Euro was not an economic decision at all. Their economy was already in step with Euroland. The Danish Krone had been pegged to the German Deutschmark for the previous eighteen years. The Danes realised the choice was primarily a political decision although their Government never spelled it out. They decided they didn't want political union within the EU, and voted accordingly.

The good news is that the UK's choice on the Single Currency will also be made by the people. It was Conservative policy at a very early stage that this key constitutional issue should be decided by Referendum, a policy hastily copied by Labour. The question is when?

Gordon Brown still pretends five economic tests have to be passed before he would approve the UK joining up. The result has to be 'clear and unambiguous'. To help his cabinet colleagues answer the question Gordon thoughtfully produced for them over 2000 pages of analysis, a total of 38 tonnes of paper by the time it reached every MP.

In fact this costly Treasury exercise ended up answering a different question. By saying that the time was not right at this moment and that the economy was still on the move, the clear implication is that even if the time were to become right in the future it could just as easily become wrong again soon afterwards.

We have been there before.

The famous five tests, originally designed to smooth the way for entry, have done the opposite. That is why for Tony Blair the five tests were always less important than the One Big Test: when will the opinion polls say he might win a referendum?

He will have a long wait.

Chapter Sixteen

Europe – wherever next?

As a history student I remember reading about the Treaty that finally signalled the end of years of carnage in Europe. Countless lives had been lost from numerous nations, and the politicians were determined that this European war had to be the last.

The year was 1648. The Treaty of Westphalia that concluded the Thirty Years' War was soon unwound. Such history would repeat itself again and again over the centuries that followed.

By 1950 Europe was in its latest mess. World War Two had finished five years earlier, but national economies were still depressed. So were the people. Most countries still had national service, with most fathers still resigned to their sons following them in fighting their natural enemies in Europe at some stage in the future. War had flared up on the continent twice within half a century: everyone hoped there would not be a third time, but had no reason to believe it could never happen again given the continent's troubled history.

For one man, hope was not enough. He cared about the future and saw the need for a radical re-appraisal of how European nations inter-acted. His name was Robert Schuman.

Schuman is described by a biographer as "a Luxemburger by birth, a German by education, and a Frenchman with all his heart." Today, we might describe him as the first true European. Elected for the first time as a member of the French House of Representatives in 1919 after the First World War, he became Minister of Finance in 1946 just after the Second. Two years later he was Foreign Minister. It was in this role that he was to make history.

He knew that the age-old rivalry between France and Germany was still intense. He also knew that the two great engines of war were coal and iron: both had to join together to make steel. France had the largest reserves of iron ore in Europe, but Germany had the coal. Each country needed what the other had: this was always a potential recipe for war.

On 9th May 1950, he called together the international press and presented what came to be known as 'The Schuman Declaration'. He proposed that Franco-German production of coal and steel as a whole should be placed under one common High Authority. The intention was that any war between France and Germany should become not merely unthinkable, but materially impossible. This was to be a first step towards 'the federation of Europe', and because it was 'open to all countries willing to take part, will lay a true foundation for their economic unification.'

It was a dramatic idea, eagerly embraced in principle by Germany as well as France. The following year, the Treaty of Paris confirmed it. The new High Authority was to be called the European Coal and Steel Community. It was the forerunner of what was to become the European Union.

Many British fondly believe they later joined a simple 'Common Market'. Initially its title was indeed the EEC, the European Economic Community. But the original political vision was always the more significant. It was clearly spelt out fully fifty years ago. It was about peace in Europe. It was indeed about unification.

The British press at the time was not enthusiastic. The leading article in one major daily paper stated firmly: 'No country which loses national control of coal and steel can retain national freedom. This threat to our sovereignty is not accidental. It is part of a deliberate and concerted attempt to force Britain into a United Europe'.

But there was to be no force. There was to be free choice, and continental Europe was clearly choosing to come together.

Six countries began to build on the work of the two, and crowned their discussions at the Treaty of Rome in 1957. Sceptical of its success, Britain didn't even bother to send a minister to participate in the debate, relying instead on a senior civil servant as an observer, one Russell Bretherton. History records that he was unimpressed by the proceedings. He apparently reported back to the UK Government that the six would probably never agree on anything; if they did agree, nothing would happen; and if anything did happen it wouldn't work. Based upon that profound analysis, Britain stayed aloof while the new Europe prospered.

Not only has it prospered economically: the European Union has succeeded in keeping the peace within itself for the second half of the twentieth century and into the twenty-first. Some sceptics say the credit for this belongs to NATO, but NATO was designed to combat external threats not stop wars between its members. The credit flows from the original Schuman vision. Mine is the first generation not to have been called upon to fight for my country. My son is the second, and takes it for granted. This is a wondrous prize, especially as it has eluded all our forbears.

All Western Europe welcomes this, though the UK has a somewhat different perspective. It is a consequence of being an island, coupled with being a major economic power. We have often fought in continental wars, but have not fought a battle inside our own homeland since Culloden in 1746. We have often landed on continental shores, but have not been invaded ourselves for a thousand years. Peace means much to us, but it means so much more to the continent.

In mainland Europe national boundaries have ebbed and flowed, with languages and tribes often having flows of their own. Most EU countries did not even exist, certainly within their current boundaries, before around 1870. Throughout the centuries, all have needed to adapt to constant change.

For us in Britain, being an island has meant that our boundaries have stayed firmly fixed. As an island, isola in Latin, the UK has remained literally isolated from the deepest effects of this continental turmoil.

Neither has our language overflowed into neighbouring lands (with the exception of Ireland – another island and another story). Our monarchy and our institutions have been challenged but have survived the centuries intact. We have evolved, but we have seen less need for radical change. We like what we have, we cherish it, and we want to hold on to it.

We continue to drive on the left side of the road. We still measure distance in miles. We continue to call our motorways M1 and M6 whereas the continent long ago moved to E numbers to signify Euro-routes. We quaff our ale in pints, and are reluctant to lose our pounds and our ounces despite continental metrication way back in Napoleonic times. We stayed loyal to the Julian calendar even when Europe switched to the Gregorian, leaving us 11 days apart for some 130 years. We rejected the continental centralism and absolutism of 'popery', preferring the protestant cause. To many Europeans we have never ceased protesting.

Some years ago I was talking with a consultant who was working for the DTI. On one particular project, he had to visit Brussels. He told me that although the cost was less than a flight to Edinburgh, a journey he did regularly without problem, the trip to Belgium had to be authorised in advance because it was 'abroad'. For many British, mainland Europe will always be abroad, a perception our continental colleagues find simply very odd.

Berliners are ever grateful of the huge role Britain played in the famous airlift, when they were encircled by a glowering Russian threat. Across communities in Belgium and the Netherlands there are war memorials proclaiming local gratitude to the British armed forces that liberated them from the Nazis. These people recognise us as Europeans, and see what we have in common. All too often we see just our differences.

These differences are not just a matter of geography and history. Our political philosophy is different too. The UK has a one-party government, except at time of war. Alternate visions are presented to the electorate, but when the votes have been counted there is only one winner and the winner takes all. The losing alternate views may still be articulated, but depending on the size of the majority the government of the day may not need to listen. Indeed some say that the current UK Prime Minister does not even listen to the cabinet.

In contrast continental governments, certainly in the last century, have generally been coalitions. For them, consensus and compromise are political facts of life. Such ruling parties, and indeed such countries, regard compromise as something positive: they have won some part of what they wanted. For the UK, compromise represents defeat: we have failed to get something that we needed. It is little wonder that the EU is so unpopular at home, and that this is not just a matter of party politics.

The much-maligned Edward Heath realised that our future lay in Europe, but this was not a universal view even within the Conservative party. When the time came for the country to choose via a vote in the House of Commons, internal party divisions were evident. Wisely, Heath decided to have a free vote. Labour MPs, under Harold Wilson, were under a three-line whip to vote against.

All parties split, but cross-party support ensured a massive majority of over a hundred. The outcome was decisive, but the fight was not over: indeed the fight has continued with varying ferocity ever since.

For many, the fight is about the preservation of the nation state. It is to save us from becoming absorbed in an apparent federalist plot, connived at by leading politicians from other EU countries, to join a United States of Europe. It is a fight not just about what Europe is now, but mainly about where Europe is heading. There are many battlegrounds in this fight.

One such battleground is the future of Regional Government. The Commission wants this throughout the EU because it could then have direct contact with the regions and bypass national Governments. Tony Blair wants it for the UK as this would mean large urban-led (and therefore Labour-led) authorities controlling what went on in the Shires.

Edmund Stoiber of Bavaria famously said: "Bavaria is my country, Germany is my nation, and Europe is my future." Bavaria has existed as a kingdom for a thousand years, whereas Germany was a recent construct of the late nineteenth century. The UK has the opposite tradition: we have had our country for a thousand years (give or take the Act of Union), whereas we have had regions such the West Midlands for but a handful of years. When I say to people I am an MEP for the West Midlands region, people ask where is that? And these are people who actually live in the region.

We have a different perspective of Europe's future, just as we have had a different past. Continental countries came together primarily to make peace: Britain signed up mainly to make money. We needed a huge home market for our trade. We had lost our empire and our captive markets: we needed Europe to mean business.

It is interesting today, looking back to the 1970's, to note how Labour at the time was so fervently against joining. This was not just the view of the then leadership: fledgling politicians and future leaders such as Tony Blair felt the same at the time. He put withdrawal from the EU as the centrepiece of his original election manifesto for Sedgefield constituency. Times do indeed move on.

The original Labour antipathy came from a belief that the EEC would be a great success and a stunning showpiece for capitalism. Socialism would be consigned to history. Such a future clearly had to be resisted. In reality that future has evolved differently. Certainly prosperity has grown rapidly, but so has the Left. In 1999, 13 out of 15 Member States had Left or Left-leaning Governments. As Governments appoint Commissioners, these too were mainly Socialist. The Left has been running Europe for years; Socialist regulations have abounded. No wonder UK Labour politicians are now such fans. No wonder so many real people in the UK feel stifled and submerged in a sea of excessive and intrusive legislation.

The majority of constituents I meet nowadays, from all political parties or none, are at best lukewarm about our membership of the EU. At worst they want out. Ask them to name the current Member States, or even their number, and they struggle. Ask them to spell out what the

EU has done for them and there is often stony silence. Ask them what their MEPs do and they have no idea – unless of course they have read this book.

Certainly the fact we were not in the EU at the beginning hasn't helped. France in particular was able to craft the rules in its own image. The European Commission was set up by the French as an exact copy of their own highly-centralised system. The European Parliament was also mirrored on the French model, even down to the uniform of the ushers or huissiers. The Common Agricultural Policy (or CAP) was set up basically to protect French farmers. Over half the EU budget goes to subsidise agriculture, although less than 5% of Europeans work on the land. Much of it goes to France but all of us pay. Real reform is utterly resisted. Even though the CAP flouts WTO rules, penalises third world export markets, and contributes to environmental damage across the EU, this waste of taxpayers' money goes on. And on.

Tony Blair maintains that we have only ourselves to blame because we weren't in the EU at the beginning: we were not there to help set the agenda. He then makes the illogical leap to suggest that therefore we have to sign up to everything now on a different agenda. If we had been there at the start, it is possible there might have been less momentum for a Single Currency. Or a harmonised Europe-wide tax system. Or a European Army. Or a European Public Prosecutor within a pan-European judicial system. To sign up to all this stuff now would simply compound our original error.

Our initial absence was indeed a grave error of judgement. We didn't see it at the time. There were many other things we didn't notice afterwards either.

In the two decades before the UK joined, the EU founding fathers moved their personnel into every level of power. We neglected this even after we joined: we provided some senior officials but failed to see the need to colonise every corridor. Secretaries and *fonctionnaires* have real power too. It has taken until now to propose reforms that will position people in future on merit rather than nationality.

We didn't notice that the European Trade Unions had themselves did notice this. They moved their people in, and also encouraged their members and supporters to become MEPs: this twin-track approach has certainly paid off for them.

We never realised there would be so many rules. We didn't register that the free movement of people, goods, capital and services simply could not happen without a mass of regulations. Officially the EU laws take the place of fifteen sets of national rules – often at the behest of industry, wanting to see a common regulatory framework. But we still see that bureaucracy rules ok. We don't of course see that we help to make these rules. We do feel, though, that we are the only country to follow them. We also feel that we should scrap a lot of them and start again.

The European Convention was set up to address exactly these sort of issues; what the EU is and should try to be; what it does and what it should not do; where it should be going and how fast. These are questions that should have been answered a long time ago, but they were never really addressed. Better late than never – always assuming the right answers emerge.

This is where the UK can be so useful. We are in Europe, but not of Europe. Our island mentality and our heritage mean that we can stand back and look at Europe more objectively. The EU certainly needs such a dispassionate gaze.

We believe the EU should aim to do less and do it better. It should look outwards, not inwards. We believe that the EU may grind to a halt in the future if it fails to define where it is going and why. Such a grinding is certain if its defined destination fails to strike a chord in the heart of the people.

Some in the UK believe fervently that as the fourth or fifth largest economy in the world we could survive on our own. Doubtless we could. But is that the issue? Is that really in our long-term interest, or indeed that of Europe? Do we want to see a large Socialist federation on our doorstep, and be in no position to curb its wilder excesses? Do we want to see our major trading partners set all the trading rules, for us to follow what we could not shape?

Do we believe that with the division of Europe finally healed, when Eastern and Central European nations are voting with large majorities to join the EU, that it is sensible to create a new division – with us alone on the outside?

Do we think that if we stopped contributing our 1.03% of GNP into the EU budget, then suddenly we would have such a stash of spare cash to spend on extra schools and hospitals? Gordon Brown has raised more than this every single year with his stealth taxes.

Do we really believe that if we came out, the Government would abruptly bin all the extra laws they have currently signed up to, so that with one bound we would be freed of all this extra red tape? Leaving the EU would not reverse this trend. A change in Government in the UK would make a difference.

My mind goes back to the time of the Referendum in 1975, when the people were to be asked whether we wanted to stay in the EEC. I attended a local Conservative meeting, addressed by a totally forgettable MP with an unforgettable message. He said that a Referendum was unconstitutional, and the best thing we could do for democracy (which in his definition meant leaving all decisions to the Houses of Parliament), was not to vote at all. I understood instantly then, as I have often understood since, why politicians were so poorly regarded.

I made my first political speech impromptu and said this advice was daft. Parliament had agreed the Referendum. It was not about the powers of Westminster but the future of the country. We needed a decisive result, with the fullest possible involvement of the electorate. We shouldn't opt out of such a decision: it was imperative we opted in. At the end of my speech I found I had opted in to the Conservative Party, all because of Europe.

The Referendum was indeed decisive, yet it for many in the UK the decision is still not final. The idea of an undefined 'ever closer union' is generally welcomed on the continent, but the British people have yet to sign up to such a European vision. Our vision of Europe, and of Britain in Europe, has always been different and clear. We have argued vigorously about it throughout these past 50 years, between political parties, within parties, with our fellow members of the EU, and inside the European Parliament. We shall doubtless go on arguing: it is our right and our role. The good news is that more and more Member States are now throwing out their failed socialist governments. The even better news is that the ex-communist candidate countries do not want a new set of Socialist shackles when they join the EU. We are no longer in the minority seeking change.

The Iraq conflict in 2003 highlighted this well, with the perceptive American jibe about France and Germany being 'Old Europe'. Such countries may have their own agenda, and it is not for us to stop them. But it is not for them to stop us and others in the enlarged EU from taking a very different route.

When General de Gaulle vetoed the UK original entry he said it was because when faced with a choice of embracing Europe or America, the UK would always choose *le grand large*, usually translated as the wide-open sea. The real choice is for Europe: whether the EU as a whole wants to be Fortress Europe – a closed highly centralised world – or to look outwards and beyond.

It will not be easy to drive for such a change, but change there must be. But if we feel progress is too slow we should never opt out. We must not let Old Europe win by default. Despite the consistent – and mutual – frustration, we should stay actively opted in and simply work with even greater intensity to shape our own vision of a positive European future.

It will never be easy.

It would be much easier if Labour and Liberal Democrat politicians voted alongside us in trying to secure it.

Chapter Seventeen

The Gravy Train

I got into politics because I was not a politician. I wasn't one of them: I was one of us.

But what am I now? To most people I became 'one of them' the day I first signed on. I am on the same gravy train as every other politician – except that the MEPs' carriages are considered to be luxury class.

Apparently the great thing about being an MEP is that you can make around £200,000 a year, or £1million in a full five-year term.

Or so people tell me.

When I respond that every MEP currently has the same salary as their national MP back home they are convinced I must be pulling both their legs and not merely one. But that is the reality, which also means that when Westminster MPs vote themselves a rise – as they seem to do fairly regularly – UK MEPs benefit simultaneously without having had to lift a finger.

The UK salary for Westminster MPs has risen in seven years from just under £32,000 a year in 1994 to over £56,000 a year by Spring 2003. This may sound a wondrously high salary to some. For those of us with a business background it actually represents a massive discount to our previous earnings: but then nobody should go into public service for financial gain.

There is no real logic for MEPs having the same salary as a back-bench Westminster MP. We have very different roles. Most back-bench MPs can have little influence over what goes on in their Parliament even if their party is in Government: MEPs from all parties have real power to shape EU law. MPs have the time to take other salaried jobs as well: MEPs generally don't, given the added inconvenience of travelling to and working in Belgium/France as well as the challenge of a relating to a vast constituency back home. Despite that the Chairman of the Parliamentary Labour Party has said that Westminster MPs are somehow so stressed that they should get stress counselling – and of course get it free.

The so-called reform of Westminster working hours has proposed that Westminster MPs in future should only work on Monday afternoons, and then only from 9am – 5pm on Tuesday and Thursday. Maybe the reason MPs are so stressed is because they already have so much time off. Generally they return from their summer holidays in mid October: in contrast, MEPs go back to work on August Bank Holiday.

I am not trying to knock an MPs' job: it is not a role I could perform at all well. We also work closely and constructively together. It is just that I question why we should get the same salaries for such very different jobs, working such very different hours. Having said that, I believe it is for our employers to determine our pay and conditions not ourselves, and our employer is and should remain Her Majesty's Government.

Although notionally MEPs from all Member States do the same job as each other, we all get very different salaries reflecting the different amounts paid to national MPs in our respective countries. As at January 2003, the monthly gross salaries per nationality were as shown in the chart opposite (in Euros, for comparative purposes):

I should add that the monthly amounts are not strictly comparable as some countries pay out 13 or 14 times a year rather than the normal 12. It is nice work if you can get it, as they say.

Member State	Gross Monthly salary in Euros	Number of months paid per year
Austria	7,500	14
Belgium	5,668	12
Denmark	5,555 (=41'368 DKR)	12
Finland	4,541	12
France	5,205	12
Germany	7,009	12
Greece	4,800	14
Ireland	5,984	12
Italy	10,974	12
Luxembourg	4,907	13
Netherlands	6,467	12
Portugal	3,448	14
Spain	2,618	14
Sweden	4,800 (= 43,200 SEK)	12
United Kingdom	7,106 (=£4,620)	12

(Source: DG III Media Monitoring & Analysis Unit)

A few years earlier, the UK MEP pay had been nearer the middle of the scale, but as the Euro weakened during 2001/2 our salary in sterling became worth more Euros. Conversely, as the Euro strengthened against the £ during 2003, we have since dropped down the rankings.

Each MEP currently pays the appropriate national taxes, which means that the differences in take-home pay of MEPs from different countries are often even wider than in the above chart.

This may all be about to change. For years attempts have been made to produce a Members' Statute whereby all MEPs should be paid the same.

In mid-2003 this was finally voted through by the Parliament to be discussed by Member States in the European Council. The suggestion now is that starting from the new five-year mandate in 2004, all MEPs from all Member States should be paid the same gross salary as each other – equal pay for equal work. This has been provisionally proposed as half the salary of a European Judge in the European Court of Justice, currently €8500/month. For the record, Conservative MEPs voted against this.

If the £/€ exchange rate had stayed at mid 2002 levels, this would have translated into a UK salary of around £62,000 a year, which would probably be the same as UK MPs by then anyway. On that basis there would probably have been little fuss from the press. But the strength of the Euro relative to the Pound by mid-2003 now means a potential pay rise to around £70,000 plus. No wonder one newspaper headlined the vote in the Parliament: 'Stronger Euro gives British MEPs £17,000 of extra gravy.' For the record we haven't got it, we are unlikely to get it, and Conservative MEPs voted against it happening at all.

The vote included the proposal that MEPs should be paid by the EU rather than the individual Member States, and also that we should all pay the same standard rate of EU Tax, which starts as low as 10%, so that we would get the same net pay too. Certainly all the Commissioners get paid the same salary on this basis, and all only pay EU tax – but then they are paid by the EU whereas we are paid by our own national Governments. I bet you didn't know that.

Countries such as the UK, Austria, Denmark, Finland and Sweden all want their national MEPs to continue pay their national tax. As we work for our country not for the EU this seems fair and reasonable. Conservative MEPs have consistently voted to pay the same tax as our constituents, but the European Parliament as a whole has voted against this by a large majority.

It is now in the hands of the Council to decide. We have also urged the Council to sort out the system of paying travel expenses which regularly and understandably hits the headlines.

Currently every MEP gets paid each week on arrival in Brussels/Strasbourg for the expenses of the journey to/from their home that they have just made. This is calculated on the basis of a full YY Economy fare airline ticket from the nearest domestic airport plus a kilometrage (same principle as mileage), to the airport from your home. However much or little you have paid for your flight, you get paid the same fixed expense allowance for each journey.

We do not, as the press often allege, travel economy and claim business. On showing proof of travel, i.e. boarding cards, we are given a fixed allowance in return. The issue is that this allowance can be much higher than the real cost of travel, given the wide availability of cut-price tickets.

What we want to see is a system whereby we are only repaid the exact costs we have incurred. Hopefully this will happen soon, though ironically it won't save the taxpayer a penny as MEPs would then fly full YY Economy fare as we are entitled to do. However, it might at least stop the media focusing on the MEPs' Gravy Train image: maybe instead they might spend time discussing what we actually do.

On top of the basic salary package we also have certain other allowances. For every day that we sign in at Brussels or Strasbourg, we are given a daily allowance worth around £155 for out-of-pocket expenses. In a full year this can be as much as £25,000 if we are there on every possible working day. It sounds as if this sum goes straight into our pockets rather than straight out of them, but then we do have to pay for accommodation in both places, plus meals (and no, we are not entertained the whole time) plus laundry, taxis etc..

Most MEPs buy or rent a flat in Brussels, as we are there three weeks out of four, and stay in a hotel in Strasbourg. Hotels are not cheap, especially in Strasbourg, where prices always seem to rise mysteriously for the few days a month that the Parliament is there.

It is possible to spend more than the allowance, though it is also possible to save a proportion of it – especially if you are prepared to slum it in a poky room some way out of town or share with one or more colleagues.

Still, any room or flat usually has to be rented at least on a twelve-month basis, if not for the full five years, so you still have to shell out for rent even when not there.

If you commit to the expense of a flat, your rental expenses are fixed. But your daily allowance income is variable depending on how many days you sign in. In other words, it pays you to be in Brussels rather than your constituency back home. Every day you are in the constituency rather than Brussels/Strasbourg it 'costs' you the £155 daily allowance which you then forfeit. That is hardly a spur to be a good constituency member – which perhaps explains why some aren't.

This daily allowance of up to £25k p.a. compares with an equivalent for Westminster MPs of around £20k. This is given to those MPs who live outside London, and is intended to cover the costs of over-nighting when in the capital.

There is another allowance that MEPs get back home though it is still paid in Euros. This is worth around £2,200 a month for 'general expenses', or frais generaux. As this is from the Parliament, and not from our employer, it has been agreed by the Inland Revenue that this is not taxable. Again, all of it is likely to be used up. It is intended to cover transport and overnight costs around the constituency, telephone and fax costs (including mobile phone bills, which soon mount up to and from Belgium & Strasbourg) plus office equipment, photocopying, rent and rates as necessary together with postage, newspapers etc.. Continental MEPs without such active constituency commitments still get the same allowance regardless, though they never get our negative press coverage. Indeed they often get no press coverage at all.

On a full year basis the £2,200 per month equates to some £26,400 per year. This compares with an Office Costs Allowance for a Westminster MP of £18,000 p.a.- though MPs can also get 3 pcs, 1 laptop, 2 printers/scanners and associated software provided free for use in Westminster and/or their constituency. MPs can also claim free 1st class train fares throughout the UK, plus mileage at a rate of over 50p/mile for travelling by car around their local constituencies. Apparently 'custom and practice' determines that no MP ever claims less than £1,000/month to cover mileage costs. I know which deal is the more generous.

The final major allowance for MEPs which again sounds eminently pocketable is a monthly Secretarial allowance worth about £100k p.a., compared with Westminster secretarial allowances of around £60k (or £70k for those with London constituencies). However, this £100k does not just have to cover administration and secretarial costs back in the UK throughout the huge regional constituency. It also has to cover research and secretarial costs in Brussels and in Strasbourg, including the copious and detailed work necessary for dealing with Reports – work that most MPs don't have to cope with out of their own resources in the House of Commons. Such costs are not cheap, especially in Brussels where tax and social security costs are even higher than in the UK - though the UK under Gordon Brown is trying to catch up fast.

No money can go to any individual secretary or researcher without a formal and detailed contract, a copy of which has to be logged with the Parliament. Every MEP is potentially subject to annual audit to cross-check that everything is hunky-dory. And quite right too. This is not just for the protection of the taxpayer, but also for the protection of MEPs who cannot then be accused of filching public funds. The newspapers must be very disappointed.

In common with MPs and Members of the House of Lords, we get free parking at many airports in the UK; we also get free transport between the European Parliament and airports serving Brussels or Strasbourg. We are offered free rail travel throughout Belgium and Luxembourg, not that we do a lot of that. Like MPs, we get free life assurance cover up to the value of four times salary if we die in service. The Parliament also reimburses medical expenses for MEPs plus spouses and dependent children.

When we finally stop being MEPs we also get two other payouts. One is six months salary, which MPs also get. The other is a life insurance payout of €15,338 (and 75 cents – every little helps)) if we have reached sixty years of age and have served two terms. If we leave after only one term, we either take the five-year surrender value, or we continue the premiums at our own expense for a further five years.

UK MEPs also share the same pension scheme as UK MPs, though as MEPs we have an additional top-up plan via the European Parliament – the equivalent of an extra voluntary-contribution scheme. We each can put in contribution ourselves of just over £500/month out of our net salary, as the payment does not qualify for tax relief, and the European Parliament puts in double the amount. This contribution has been carefully set by someone somewhere somehow as 13% of 40% of the basic salary of a Judge.

At the age of 60 (or on retirement as an MEP, whichever comes later), this additional scheme should cough up a pension of €1150/month for an MEP who has served a single five-year mandate. Subject to the value of the Euro, this should be worth around £8,500/year, which is quite handy. For two such mandates, the total pension would rise to seventeen grand a year, which would be even handier. It is linked to inflation, being expressed as 3.5% of 40% of a Judge's salary for each full year of MEPdom up to a maximum of 20 years. It could be worth even more if the Judges get a raise.

I personally think that these Judges are very underpaid……

Certainly if you add up all the money coming in, £200,000/year looks realistic as income. But much of the incoming becomes outgoing almost immediately. It has to cover not just the cost of employing staff but also the costs of travelling and living abroad. When you take away all these expenses you end up with a dramatically lower figure: this of course never hits the headlines. If you had any business sense you would stay in business where the financial rewards are so much higher.

But that is not why I and my colleagues signed up. I joined to fight for Conservative values, and to fight for less red tape. I wanted to stand up for business, for jobs, for freedoms, and to change European law. I wanted to try and make a difference, however small, and I believe I have done that. Indeed my Conservative MEP colleagues can say the same: many have done more, and I claim no records. I have had much to learn.

The learning curve has been steep and fast. I have learnt much about the strengths of the EU as well as its weaknesses, and have tried to spread this knowledge as widely as I could. I have learnt how to help people, at individual and company level, in ways I never thought possible. I have learnt of the massive damage socialism is doing to the prosperity of Europe, and how it is not so much the 'un-elected Brussels bureaucrats' but our very own UK Labour MEPs who are making it so much worse.

I have also learnt, to my very deep regret, that the Prime Minister has no coherent strategy whatever for playing a positive role for the UK while claiming a positive role in Europe. This was immediately evident when Tony Blair signed up to the Social Chapter without even asking for anything in return, an amateurishness still regarded with disbelief by other Member States. It was transparent when he refused to challenge seriously the continuing ban by France on British beef. It is constantly re-inforced every time Old Labour MEPs are given free rein to pursue the European Socialist agenda rather than the national interest. Six different UK Ministers for Europe within six years also doesn't help.

Our partners in the EU are very aware that Tony Blair has little idea how the EU works, and doesn't know that he doesn't know. He is so concerned to be liked by other countries that standing up for his own comes a distant second. The candidate countries in particular look to the UK to provide leadership within the EU as a counterweight to the old Europe of France and Germany. It is up to us to provide it. There will be much to repair when Conservatives return to Government.

I have had the opportunity to meet many remarkable people. Together with the rest of the MEP team I have been able to represent my country and my home region at the highest level. The reward in terms of a real sense of achievement has been greater than I could ever have hoped, though the financial reward – despite public perception – has been limited as expected.

It has been a great privilege to ride this particular train. I would not have missed this opportunity for anything. But I do miss the real world, which already seems a lifetime away. I vividly resent the intrusion that public service in this role and at this level makes into private life. I am concerned that my BT Friends and Family telephone bill highlights the fax line to Brussels as my closest personal contact. I am not amused that the grandchildren refer to me as Belgian Grandpa because I seldom see them.

At times too I feel distant from the political debate back home. One of our major missions as Conservative MEPs has been to keep a check on the Commission and stop it becoming an over-mighty executive – an issue that needs to be constantly addressed. People still peddle the view that 'Brussels' is taking away powers from Westminster. Meanwhile the powers of Westminster continue to be massively eroded every day, not by Brussels but by an over-mighty UK Prime Minister who sees the Houses of Parliament as a tiresome irrelevance. This issue needs to be addressed with even greater vigour too.

In early 2003 I was re-selected to stand for a second five-year term starting in 2004. This time I am Number One on the Conservative list for the region, so barring accidents I can safely say I should be an MEP until 2009. But I do not foresee a third term to follow. Ten years will be gruelling enough – which means there will then be at least one vacancy.

So I do urge readers to put their own names forward, especially if they come from the real world, care about the issues, and want to roll back the smother of socialism. There remains serious work to be done. Previous political experience is absolutely not necessary. Knowledge of Pork Scratchings may be desirable, but is not compulsory either.

After all, clearly anyone can become an MEP these days.